FOR HEAVEN'S SAKE

James S Wood

Centre for Scottish Studies
University of Aberdeen

First published 1989

ISBN 0 906265 12 6

Printed in Great Britain by BPCC AUP Ltd, Aberdeen
Member of BPCC Ltd.

CONTENTS

EDITOR'S PREFACE

James Wood was born in Portknockie, Banffshire in 1908. After primary education there he went to Fordyce Academy, at that time a school with a great reputation throughout Scotland. In 1925, he became a student at the University of Aberdeen and graduated with a degree in English, followed by a three years Divinity course at Christ's College. While there he volunteered to go to Jamaica as tutor to the Divinity students. He then spent a term at Woodbrooke, one of the Selly Oak colleges. He was minister in Kingston, Jamaica for almost a year before moving to the country where he trained the students, as well as looking after two Churches and a Boys' Home.

Some years later the Church decided that the students should be trained at the Methodist Caenwood College in Kingston, and Mr Wood became a lecturer there as well as becoming minister of St Paul's Church. When the Principal of the College was called back to England, Mr Wood took over the post. Students of several denominations were trained at Caenwood.

In 1938 Mr Wood returned to Scotland, and for domestic reasons decided to remain there. In 1939 he married Annie Richard of Wick and shortly after was called to the parish church at Insch, but making it clear that it was his intention to volunteer as a chaplain when the opportunity arose. He joined up in April 1941 and after training at Chester, was posted to an artillery unit in the Isle of Wight, then to a searchlight unit, and thereafter briefly to a commando training camp. Being a keen mountaineer, he volunteered to serve in the 52nd Lowland (Mountain) Division. He was first with the Glasgow Highlanders and then with the 7/9th Royal Scots with whom he trained for mountain warfare before the successful invasion of Walcheren in 1944. Some time after that he was posted to a mountain battalion at home before being demobbed in 1946.

James Wood was called to Newtonmore in 1947, and from there, after some six years, to the South (now St Marks) Church in Aberdeen. He was there for twenty years, retiring in 1973. In 1972 he received the honorary title of Doctor of Divinity from his *alma mater* Aberdeen University. During his ministries, he broadcast several hundred times on television and radio (Home and World Service), an opportunity which James regarded as a wonderful extension to his work. After one set of broadcasts, he replied to 700 letters, mostly from people in trouble.

After retiring, he became a lecturer in Christ's College, was reponsible for the teaching of lay missionaries, and later for some years, was the College librarian. James and Annie have three children, Michael, Colin and Margaret.

As can be seen, James Wood has had a varied and full life in his ministry. It should be said that this is not a complete autobiography, rather a sketchbook, with a brief account of the various fields he served in and some of the people he encountered. His anecdotal and often humorous reminiscences recounted in *For Heaven's Sake* deserve to reach a wide public, as not only are they extremely entertaining, but also carry a deeper message for us all.

J.S. Smith (Editor)

AUTHOR'S ACKNOWLEDGEMENTS

My warm thanks are due to my sister-in-law, Ray Richard for her flawless typing of my original manuscript, to my dear friend Dr Ronald Selby Wright for his encouragement and his generous introduction, and to my son Michael for his unstinted help over a long period of time, not forgetting the Editor, Dr John Smith who has spent hours of his precious time on this little book.

The book is dedicated to Annie, Michael, Colin and Margaret.

Also by James Wood: *The Wind on the Hill* (poems)

FOREWORD

My only criticism of this quite delightful book is that it is not long enough. Taking account of the writer's full and varied life, one would have liked more. His career?... missionary in the West Indies, highland parson, city minister, Army padre (to a ski battalion), university lecturer, librarian, broadcaster, chaplain to the Scottish fishing fleet, etc. and all 'for heaven's sake'. All who know padre Wood could add many stories not here included... how he stopped a whole battalion from swearing, living in tents in the snow, by putting up a notice which read... The Padre would remind everyone that while these tents are snowproof, rainproof and windproof, they are NOT soundproof. Or the time at early dawn on a mountain top, he was asked by General Sir Neil Ritchie "What did you do in peace time soldier"? He simply removed the sweatrag from his neck to reveal a dog collar, a white woollen one knitted to his khaki pullover by his wife... But I can't go on. Padre Wood was to many in peace and war, an understanding friend and a wise counsellor. Above all a good family man with Michael, Colin, Margaret and the never-aging Annie. I have been proud to share his friendship, with many others. And it is good to know that this book will enable him to share his gifts with so many more

> That gift of his from God descended
> Ah friend, what gift of man's does not.

Ronald Selby Wright
Queen's House
Moray Place
Edinburgh

FOREWARNING!

This little book does not consciously set out to instruct or entertain; yet it may do both. The reader may learn something new, if that is possible, about human behaviour and human relationships. And he may well be amused by the situations which arise as one specific being, a clergyman, confronts a variety of his fellow sinners. By the way he reacts to these situations, by his assessment of the people involved, the writer will inevitably reveal something of himself, will pass judgement on himself, will sometimes annoy and hopefully sometimes earn approval, although he does not seek to avoid the one or court the other.

A teenager once told me she thought a minister was a man who should love everybody. And of course she was right; he has a directive so to do. But while I have tried hard throughout my ministry to carry out this directive, to love all men, I must confess that unavoidably I have had dealings with not a few people whom I found it very hard to *like*. The best I could do was to be tolerant and patient at least to a point, and to exercise my sense of humour, a God-given supplement to love. I have no doubt whatsoever that when I have clearly disliked certain individuals, the feeling has been reciprocated, and I do not blame anyone for that. "Beware when all men speak well of you" is a dictum I have had to resort to for comfort from time to time.

I lay no claim to sainthood unless it be the negative brand of the man who, having read through the Ten Commandments said "Well, at least I have never made a graven image". So to my knowledge, if I have not fulfilled all the obligations of love and charity, I have not deliberately hurt anyone although, as will appear, I have been greatly tempted to retaliate, with verbal or even physical violence, on more than one occasion! I would like to think however that, on the whole, like Burns,[1] I have "gently scanned my brother

1. Quote from Burns ... *Ae Fond Kiss.*

man" and, aware of my own, that my attitude to human failings had invariably been Chaucerian, with no undertones of malice or venom.

Now, no minister, parson or priest must ever betray a confidence, and you will certainly find no such betrayal in these pages, although the people and the situations herein described are real. Such disclosures as there may be are about myself and, with her permission, about my unpaid assistant, my wife. Oh yes, and without their permission, about my defenceless children. If there be an archangel who sits in judgement on books I hope he will pardon me for my sins of omission (which might have been of greater interest to the reader) as well as for my sins of commission, some of which are shamelessly recorded here.

A colleague of mine once asked me to review his autobiography remarking "I don't think it will sell well; there's no scandal in it". Nor is there here, although some folk may well describe my conduct, on occasion, as scandalous. So be it. I certainly have no doubt that some of my fellow clergymen will say I have over-exposed the profession. Others, the laymen, may say I have been too reticent, that I might have lifted the veil a bit more. In reply I might use the words with which St Augustine concluded his greatest work "Let those who think I have said too little, or those who think I have said too much, forgive me. And let those who think I have said just enough join me in giving thanks to God".[2]

IN THE BEGINNING

It was a splendid day, a day of tempest and turbulence, a day after my own heart. The sun shone from an infinity of blue. A few wispy lace-thin cloud-curtains, torn from the high casements of heaven, were blown to tatters before finally disappearing in the upper air. From the Caithness shore an endless herd of wild white horses raced across the wind-ravaged prairie of the Moray Firth, shattering themselves on the rocks far below us. A convoy of cormorants, the hover-craft of the bird world, skimmed effortlessly into the wind,

2. Augustine's greatest work ... *City of God*.

over the broken water. Above, behind and below us, gulls and terns wheeled and spiralled, screaming their exultation. A young fisherwoman yachted past us, her skirts ballooning like a voluminous spinnaker, her clothes-basket almost torn from her hands.

"A great day to be alive in" shouted Bill. We had to shout to be heard. "A super day" I yelled back, as we chiselled our way into the wind along the narrow cliff-top road. Bored with two years confinement in an office, polishing his trousers-seat on a bank-clerk's stool, Bill was leaving in two days time for Hawaii. So this would be our last walk together for some time, the last of many shared since schooldays. I had put off until now giving Bill a piece of news which I knew would shock him although I didn't think his reaction would be quite so violent. Meanwhile we walked on, our conversation minimised by the wild orchestration of wind and wave. Words were being blown to shreds even before bridging the short gap between us, so I pointed to a disused coastguard hut in the near distance and without expending any further lungpower we carved our way through the gale till we reached its shelter. We entered, closing the door quickly behind us. It was like turning down an overloud TV set while still retaining the picture, for through the wide window we could see the frothing firth and the flying spin-drift, the gleaming wings of the sea-fowl and the blue shapes of the distant hills. "There's a picture to take with you to Hawaii" I said to Bill once I got my breath back. "Aye", he said, "something to remember right enough". "But you'll have the great rollers sweeping in on Diamond Head, and the surfriders, and the hula hula girls, and all that" I consoled him. "I've no doubt there'll be compensations" he replied. "But your're going to miss all this too when you take up your London job. The Times, isn't it?" 'No, it was to have been the Daily Mail" I replied. "What do you mean, *was* to have been?" asked Bill. "I'm not going to London now. I've changed my plans". "Thinking of working with a local paper perhaps, or maybe freelancing?" conjectured Bill. "No" I said "It's a bigger change than that. I'm taking a course in divinity". "You're doing what?" he yelled. "Yes, I'm going to be a minister"! He stared at me as if I were mentally unbalanced. "I don't believe it" he groaned "I just don't believe it. You, with a good English degree and all set up for an interesting career in journalism, *you* a minister. Why this confounded change of plan, for heaven's sake?" "You've said it Bill, it's for Heaven's sake. I find it hard to explain. Some time back I had a sudden urge, a call, if you like, to do this. I've tried to reason myself out of it but I can't".

"You're plumb crazy" said Bill. "Do you know what the French say? There are three sexes, men, women and clergymen—an emasculated profession like that is not for a fellow like you. Has the adrenalin stopped flowing or have you had a rush of blood to the head? Have you had a word with your doctor, or better still, your psychiatrist?" "It's no use Bill" I smiled. "My mind is made up". "I just can't believe it" he muttered. "I just can't imagine you gowned and banned, laying forth to a congregation of ancient crones and long-faced greybeards. The very idea makes me laugh. And what about Annie, what's she saying about this volte-face of yours? Does she want to break off the engagement?" "She's quite happy I assure you" I said. "Like Ruth in the Old Testament she says 'Where thou goest I will go' ".

"You're taking advantage of a young girl, that's what" rejoined Bill. "Does she realise what she's being condemned to. Beautiful, elegant Annie. She might as well take the veil and go into a convent, and what a waste of femininity that would be". "It's not so bad as that" I countered. "She'll have a varied and interesting life". "Varied life, my foot" he retorted. "Organising bazaars and sales of work and women's outing ... that's no life for a girl like Annie. What's more she'll spend much of her time dusting and sweeping a gloomy fifteen-roomed Victorian manse, and from your miserable salary you won't be able to afford a once-a-week home-help". I let him rampage on. The turbulence of the outside world was matched by the tumult within the hut. Bill was now a volcano in full eruption, his verbal lava overwhelming but not destroying my fire-proof resolution.

"Anything more Bill?" I asked in dulcet tones. "Plenty more" he raged. "You'll not even be able to keep Annie in nylons and she'll have to change her smart shoes for buttoned boots. It's a crying shame I tell you, to condemn a girl like that to an existence entirely devoid of excitement and adventure, and all the fun a lovely healthy young girl has the right to expect. And you ... YOU ... with all your vim and vigour and versatility to be spending your life in a backwater. For heaven's sake man, think again before it's too late." "Bill" I said quietly "I have thought again and again and again, and I am convinced it is for heaven's sake I'm doing this. And what's more, Annie is convinced as well".

"I see it's no good trying to dissuade you" he growled. "No doubt you'll be happy in a tame sort of way. Well, you can have your hallelujahs. I'm for the hula hulas". "Right Bill" I said, "We'll leave it at that". We reminisced for a bit and then stepped out into the wind-riven world. The gale had reached a new crescendo. The gulls were screaming their defiance. The firth was a boiling cauldron and the sky still marvellously blue.

That evening my mind went back a few years, recollecting teenage adventures we had shared and enjoyed and it suddenly occurred to me, with some amusement that Bill, not I, might have been the parson, judging by his early susceptibilities. A religious revival had swept the northeast when we were both about thirteen. Conversions were the order of the day. Publicans as well as sinners were affected. Jake Simpson who had made his pile off immoderate imbibing, poured the fragrant contents of his pub down the public drain watched by a group of his former customers who, though now converted themselves, watched the wasteful procedure without any obvious enthusiasm. At least they did not applaud as in all conscience they should have done.

Habits of a lifetime were changed during that period. Fishermen threw away their claypipes and bogie-roll tobacco. Youngsters put their mouth-organs in the fire or the bucket. Everything even faintly associated with pleasure was ruthlessly discarded. Bill and I, with many more of our age group, attended a series of meetings addressed by an ardent evangelist whose sermons were redolent of brimstone. He made it very clear that unless we gave up our sinful ways the Almighty would make it very hot for us indeed, emphasising that the heat would last a very long time. I can still remember wondering how any human constitution could possibly survive the temperatures hinted at for any length of time, far less than for eternity. Anyhow, threats and appeals moved me not. I was determined not to give up my evil ways whatever they were. I certainly had no intention of destroying my beloved mandolin which was such a source of worldly pleasure to me. I wouldn't even have swopped it for a harp.

With Bill it was a different story. He was 'converted' three times in one week and couldn't understand how I remained impervious to all appeals to mend my ways. He was convinced that mine would be a pretty dreadful destiny. But, saved and unsaved we still went around together. In fact, at the height of the revival just after Bill's third 'conversion' he agreed to come with me on an egg-hunting expedition to the Hill of Maud where we had gone in our jointly unregenerate days, to the voluble discomfiture of the blackheaded gulls. "I'll just come for company of course" said Bill. As we wandered through the heather he lustily sang a favourite redemption hymn 'Throw out the life-line' and then suddenly he gave a shout from away back in time, a shout that had the pagan sound of his pre-reformation days... "Here's a nest wi' three eggs". I, of course, still unconverted, could harry the nest without a twinge of conscience. Then off we'd go again, Bill singing soulfully to the screaming descant of scores of angry gulls. 'Though your sins be as scarlet, they shall be as white as snow' momentarily forgetting Messrs Moody and Sankey to give another unregenerate yell, of pure pre-revival quality... "Here's another nest wi' twa". Again under his direction I did the harrying. And so it went on with Bill singing the songs of salvation, alerting me from time to time to the location of eggs with which in his saved condition he could not lay hands on. That day I not only had to plunder the nests, I had to carry the eggs, twenty of them, on the five mile return walk. Arrived back, Bill said with condescending piety "I think I could accept ten eggs as a ... as a sin offering", a phrase he had picked up in the revival hall. I readily handed over half the spoil. So saint and sinner shared the booty of that bright afternoon on the Hill of Maud. May the Lord forgive us both.

Two days after our clifftop walk I saw Bill off on the first stage of his long journey to Oahu. As the train moved out I said "Aloha", adding for good measure ... "Hula Hula". Bill responded with a hearty "Hallelujah".[3] That was the end of an era and in no time, it seemed, my divinity course was begun and finished, my apprenticeship served and I was in my first parish. A backwater, Bill had suggested, but the sea, Annie and I were launched out on was far more turbulent than we could have foreseen. And Annie was to have all the fun which Bill had said was her right, though not the sort of fun he visualised. He meanwhile was polishing the seat of his trousers on another stool in a sugar estate office, far away from

3. Bill spent most of his life in Hawaii.

the twanging of the guitars and the voluptuous swinging of grass skirts.

THE BLESSED ISLAND

You have read or heard, no doubt, of men who said they had a definite "call" to the ministry, as if they had a direct message from God. Such men, I am sure, are sincere. I must say I was aware of no such call. In fact I had no intention of being a minister at all. My university degree (in English) prepared me for the profession of my choice, journalism. Then I met a Christian whose life challenged me and to my own amazement I suddenly decided on a divinity course, already referred to, which meant several more years at College. Beyond the end of that course, I did not dare to look. However, when the time came, I had made up my mind on one thing, I did not want to begin my ministry in the homeland, and so I applied for several vacancies abroad, in Canada (Prince Edward Island, home of Anne of Green Gables!) in Amsterdam, in Rio Tinto in Spain. All these posts had already been filled. What then? The "call" came unexpectedly from one of our senior missionaries in the West Indies. He spoke at a final year college dinner, stressing the need of a man to take charge of our College in Jamaica, the Blessed Island. I immediately volunteered. Perhaps I was thought to be somewhat insular so the Church authorities sent me to the Quaker College of Woodbrooke for a term. That was a great experience for there I made contact with men of various nationalities, including West Indians. I just missed meeting Ghandi who had been there the term before.

Then, before I knew it, I was on the high seas to the Caribbean, to a new world and a new life. I fell in love with the lush and lovely island from the moment I saw it in the blue distance. Its palm-fringed shores, its blue-green mountains were, it seemed to me, a foretaste of paradise. And I fell in love with the people, their old world courtesy, their happy heartedness, the warmth of their welcome to a stranger.

The population was an amalgam of black, brown and white, with several thousand Chinese and East Indians. The presence in Jamaica of the last mentioned needs to be explained. After slavery was abolished (1837) the liberated slaves were not inclined to go on working on the estates of their former masters and owners. So indentured labour had to be imported from India. Hence the Indian presence there, with Hindi-speaking natives. With so many nations represented on the island, there was no race-relations problem. Such colour-barrier as there was, existed between the light-brown natives and the black population. The brown were inclined to think themselves superior to the black, who had a great sense of humour. "God made the white people" they would say "and God made the black people. But who made you? You are neither the one thing nor the other". I must confess I had a particular fondness for the pure negro especially in the country area where my work lay.

That work consisted of being minister to two Churches, a home for thirty delinquent boys, and a college for training native ministers, I being the entire staff! It was a busy life and a happy one. The climate, 2000 feet up in orange and banana country, was exceptionally fine. My predecessor as a young minister in Scotland, had been very delicate. His doctor told him that if he could find work in the West Indies he might add a few years to his life-span. He took the doctor's advice and ministered for fifty years in the Charge I took over, and lived another fifteen years in Scotland, in retirement. So much for the climate.

Hurricanes were not infrequent in the island, but in his half century in the parish, my predecessor had never experienced one. I, however, was to receive an elemental welcome. On the first evening of my arrival I was standing at the door of the old manse when a thick fog descended which, dramatically and frighteningly, turned blood-red. I felt something unusual in the wind (though there was no wind). I was right, a hurricane swept over my part of the island, and the morning, when the mist lifted, presented a scene of frightful agrarian destruction. It was as if a diabolical giant had spitefully uprooted all the trees, banana and bamboo, and had strewn them around. Little native dwellings were unroofed or flattened. The corrugated iron sheets covering my outhouse disappeared into the air like pieces of paper. The garage was blown in on top of my Ford. A foretaste of Paradise, I thought, when I first saw the island. Now this was a foretaste of the other place, certainly a picture of Paradise Lost.

The natives were philosophical, even cheerful, amidst all this destruction. I didn't expect anyone to be at Church my first Sunday. The building, with its roof half-lifted off was crowded, despite many of the people having to walk several miles. The new minister had to be properly welcomed. It was touching and heartwarming. I could not think of a suitable opening hymn for such an occasion and such a situation so I left the choice to them. "What shall we sing?" I asked. One young negro woman up front immediately said "Mek we sing the Magnificat ministah" and that was what we sang, "My soul doth magnify the Lord ..." What a choice after a terrifying night of storm, but I was to find this typified the spirit of the people, their courage, their faith, their refusal to lie down to a simple thing like a hurricane.

Some of my weddings were unusual, to say the least. It must be remembered that during slavery, slaves were forbidden to marry but encouraged to cohabit and produce more slaves. So I found numerous couples living together in perfect fidelity but unmarried, and with several children. I could not condemn such a relationship as sinful, but I suggested to a number of couples that they should have a simple Church ceremony when I would ask God's blessing on their partnership and their families. This was warmly agreed to so that I conducted not a few of these "blessing services", with the children present. They were happy occasions.

Many of the folk were poor but they always wanted things done decently. So to help them out I would buy a white linen suit for the "groom" (cost 10/-), purchase an inexpensive ring and have a cake baked for the reception afterwards. I left the "brides" to fend for themselves sartorially. And they appeared simply yet beautifully attired for the "wedding" service.

Besides my Churches I had several little meeting-houses to look after and in these held brief, early prayer-meetings for the folk on their way to work on their bits of land. They would leave their machettes and mattocks outside and enter the simple building very reverently. I shall never forget some of their prayers—"O Lord, bless our young minister, for him just a boy". "O Lord, we are all sinners, make our minister a broom to sweep us clean out". "O Lord, we are weak, prop us up in all our leanin' places".

In time of sorrow I have never seen greater faith than I found in these untutored country negroes. I still remember calling to see a black Elder who, in one week, had lost his wife, his eldest son and his only daughter. What could I say to him? I was immature and spiritually inadequate and knew it. But I prayed with him as best I knew how. When I finished, he looked at me out of blue eyes that saw much further into the depths of God's caring love and compassion than did mine. "Thank you minister" he said. "I know that my Redeemer liveth and that in His good time I shall see my loved ones again". I had come to teach such people—what presumption. Contact with them deepened my spiritual life far more than my theological tutors had ever done.

They were not all saints, by any means, as I was to find out. Around the manse I had some 30 acres, mostly in sour oranges. At the edge of the ground, some way from the house, there was a grove of trees and among them a particularly fine and valuable tamarind.[4] Once, returning from three days in the city, I went for a walk round the property. To my sorrow I found that the splendid tamarind had been felled, and stripped ready to take away. Naturally I could not stand guard on it yet I wanted to prevent its removal. So I took a machette and along the length of the tree, in deeply incised letters, I cut the commandment—"Thou shalt not steal". The tamarind was never touched again.

For a time I was in the city, in charge of a church, and a theological college. Life was very different here. For one thing the people were different. In my country Churches the congregations were black, without exception. In the town, sitting in the same Church pew, I would have black, brown, white and Chinese, with no feeling of apartheid whatsoever. I was inevitably caught up in situations that could not have arisen in the country. Once, by sheer chance, I escaped a beating up, by men of my own colour at that! We had an English regiment stationed partly in the city, partly in a military camp high up on a nearby mountain. One evening there was a drunken punch up and a black man had fatally assaulted a soldier. When the news got around a number of the soldiers went berserk. They beat up anyone they could lay hands on, irrespective of colour. They stopped cars and tramcars and wounded quite a number of people. It so happened I was driving through a poorer part of the town not knowing what had happened and was happening.

4. Tamarind ... a large tropical tree. Caesalpiniaceous.

I came across a soldier lying half conscious by the roadside, and managed to get him into my old Ford, with the intention of driving him to the military camp. A few minutes later I was stopped by a mob of the rioting soldiers and would have suffered the fate of so many people that night. When it was discovered I had one of their comrades in the car I was not only granted immunity, I was given a military escort to the camp, and thereafter to my house.

In 1938 there were widespread riots throughout the city. The reason on this occasion was the general low rate of pay. I must say my sympathies were with the people and I said so from the pulpit. Now, it so happened that the island governor died at the height of the riots. It was decided that he be buried at sea. As a representative of my own particular denomination I was cited to be present at the sad ceremony. The coffin was taken some ten miles out to sea in a light cruiser. It was a calm and lovely day. The Service, conducted by a Church of England dignitary was very moving. No one could have foreseen what was to happen. The heavy bronze coffin, covered by a Union Jack was slid along a protruding plank which was then tilted seaward. On its descent the coffin turned over and when it hit the sea the lid burst open. Fortunately the body was weighted and sank immediately but the coffin itself floated on the surface for quite a time. The mischievous story got about in the city that the governor, though a good and able man but not popular, had not died at all, and that the coffin had been filled with bricks. The governor, it was said, had been spirited away. Because of the trouble prevailing, this was widely believed. So much for sensational journalism. However, having been present at the Service, I was able to tell my people what really happened.

One of my interesting visits was to a little Church out on the Palisadoes. There I found a somewhat astonishing thing—the actual drinking mug of the pirate-cum-governor, Henry Morgan, being used as a flagon for the Communion wine. The handle of the flagon was the whistle he would blow when he wanted more rum. A case of sublimation if ever there was one.

My most enduring memory of the Blessed island will always be the splendid quality of life of the simple God-fearing negro people. They had such courage, such faith, such wisdom, such a sense of humour. One of the loveliest things I ever heard were words spoken by an untutored black woman. She had ten children and cared for them very dearly. One day I called to see her and found yet another child present, not a new baby but a pretty little girl of two. "Is this a neighbour's child?" I asked. "No ministah" she said. "I have adopted her". Astonished, I said "You had ten children of your own, and you go and adopt another one". Then she said, with a smile, "Ministah, I have more love in my heart than ten children can use up". I felt humbled in the presence of such a love.

I had in one of my country Churches a poor black widow in her seventies—incorrigibly cheerful she was. As there was no pension then, she had to work her own little piece of land to stay alive. She walked four miles to Church every Sunday. One day I went to see her. She was hoeing her ground. "Tell me, Miss Anderson" I said "Why are you always so contented?" She laughed and said—"Well, ministah, its like this. When I'm well and things is going well, an there's enough food in the house, I thank the Lord. When I'm not so well, and things are not so good, and there's little food in the house, I thank the Lord all the same". "I know how to be abased and to abound" said St Paul. He would have heartily approved of this poor brave soul. How much we ministers have to learn from those we seek to teach.

My term in the Blessed Island finished all too soon and, after a few months spent in surveying the home front, I was settled in a Scottish parish.

OUR ABODE

Annie's face fell when first she saw the Manse, our future home. It sprawled and rambled over half an acre of ground, with no architectural feature to command it. "Well" I said, as cheerfully as I could, "what do you think of it?" "It could hardly be advertised as 'This desirable residence' " was Annie's reply, "But before I say any more, let's have a look inside"—a look inside was a hopeful understatement. It turned out to be a voyage of exploration and discovery, for there were eighteen rooms, not counting cubby holes and deep dark cupboards. Annie gasped at the extent of the kitchen with its floor of Caithness slabs and its vast ancient range. "You could roast an ox on that" she said. "Maybe we will" I replied.

"Maybe we will". We discovered there were two separate staircases. "Well" said my dear wife, "That at least was a thoughtful provision. If ever we fall out we can each lead a separate existence without the parish knowing a thing about it". In the event we never had to resort to that; we maintained a reasonably amicable relationship throughout the years. In fact we were very happy, arguments and all.

I found that the original manse was average for the period, eleven rooms in all. But one of my predecessors, in the dim Ecclesiastical past, found it inadequate. It seems his favourite verse in the Bible was 'Be fruitful and multiply', and he was a literalist. In fact he studied the multiplication table with such assiduity that the old house, like an overflowing granary, was bursting at the beams with the fruits of his labours. So he applied to the heritors for an extension to the house. They were indignant, the more so when they discovered the reason for his request. "Had he spent more time in his study" said one of them, "this need would never have arisen". The heritors unanimously agreed to turn down his application. The godly man, however, would brook no refusal. He wasn't, he said, going to farm out any of his poor children, so he took the heritors to law and won his case, which occupies about one hundred pages in the legal annals of the Church. "No wonder he needed two staircases" said Annie, "and just fancy, eighteen plates of porridge every morning. I might have coped with that, but certainly not with the weekly washing". "Oh" I said, "a couple of servant lassies would have done the chores". "And what about the grass?" asked Annie. "We'll have sixteen acres won't we? Do you expect me to mow that lot?" "No, no" I said, "in the old days the minister kept a man to look after the glebe—but we'll rent it out as pasture". "Thank heaven for that" said Annie fervently.

We went from the dwelling to the outhouses—a byre for six cows, a stable for four horses, a henhouse, a hayshed and a loft where the minister's "man" used to sleep. "Don't worry" I said to Annie, "We can plant a row of trees between this lot and the house". "TREES", said Annie in disbelief—"Will we be staying here that long?" "Well" I said "quick-growing shrubs at any rate". "I'll water them every day" said Annie. Actually we grew to like the old place. We shut off nine rooms with the cupboards and skeletons thereof and furnished the rest with functional if not elegant furniture, bought at local roups and auction sales. We had one magnificent, high-backed, buttoned, red velvet, five seater settee which cost us ten shillings. With bright paint and cheery wallpaper we soon transformed the Victorian darkness into Georgian light.

Oh, and we had a garden too, half an acre surrounded by an eight foot stone wall. A good idea, I thought, the casual visitor won't see whether it is a barren wilderness or a fruitful vineyard. I must say I didn't like the one narrow gate, a dislike later fully justified. I planted a few things but with poor results. "The soil must be lacking in some necessary ingredient" said Annie. "Why not send a sample to the city agricultural research centre for analysis?" I agreed and did so, asking "What does this soil need to make it productive?" The answer was terse and to the point—"A lot of hard-digging". So there was no easy way out. "At least the damson tree thrives" said Annie "and the rhubarb".

But the real source of trouble was neither the house nor the garden; it was the glebe. We had that rented out to Jonathan Clark. We wouldn't have wished for a heartier tenant or a worse husbandman. He named Annie the Flower of the Glen. "We never had sic a bonnie lass in the manse". I agreed with him on that score. But behind all his blarney and bonhomie I began to sense a *je ne sais quoi* of indifference to his obligations as a tenant. The terms of his lease stated quite clearly that all fences be kept in good repair and the glebe itself be properly maintained. Alas, I found the fences in a shocking state and the glebe had the finest crop of thistles and nettles I had ever seen. This just didn't accord with Jonathan's overt piety. Any time he saw me in the distance he would start singing a hymn, pretending to be taken by surprise at my nearer approach. His favourite hymn was "We plough the fields and scatter ..." Came the day when I decided to talk to him, and in the friendliest possible way to discuss his failings as a tenant, the neglected fences, and the state of the glebe. He never raised an eyebrow. "Dinna ye worry, minister" he said. "I'll soon attend to all that". Months passed and nothing happened. I talked to him again and received the same assurance. "He was just getting round to it". A further lapse of weeks brought no change. Another talk. "You're a patient man, minister, and patience is a virtue, ye ken. But give me two more weeks and you'll have no further cause for complaint". But nothing happened. The fences were now almost flat on the ground, and the thistles and nettles were rampaging triumphantly over the glebe. Then something catastrophic happened; six of Jonathan's cows got in through the garden gate and ate all my cabbages and cauliflower I had managed to grow by dint of hard work, and with the added help of manure, kale too and everything edible. They ate the lot. The beasts were so swollen they could not get out by the way they came in. The only other way was over the eight foot wall and I couldn't imagine the cows attempting that. I was really angry. I sent for Jonathan and as he strolled down the avenue I could hear him singing "All things bright and beautiful".

"Anything wrong, minister?" he said, as he came up to me. "Just that six of your cattle have ruined my vegetable garden" I said icily. "That's a pity" he replied, "Poor beasts. What with a' these thistles and nettles taking over the grass on the glebe, they must have been hungry". "Well" I said, "just come into the garden and see what your 'poor beasts' have been up to". There stood the kine barely able to move and I swear there was more honest guilt on their bovine faces than on Jonathan's. "We'll need to get them oot" was all he said. "How?" I asked. "Through the gate, of course". "With their stomachs swollen like that?" I asked. "How did they get the elephants out of the ark" he queried, with an impudent grin. "Well, well, we'll just have to shove them out. Maybe that's what Noah and his sons did". It proved a major exercise and maybe not too humane. The cattle would become firmly wedged between the gateposts. They mooed like mad as we put our backs to their not too immaculate sterns. "Oh, that his too solid flesh would melt" I grunted. "What was that?" asked Jonathan. "Shakespeare" I said. At last the herculean task was completed. We were both soaked in sweat. "You must have had a lot of fine cabbage" said Jonathan. "Enough to do all summer and through the winter" I replied. "Never mind" he remarked consolingly "I'll bring you two bags of tatties to make up for them. And after all, you've plenty manure in your garden now". "Will you attend to the fences now?" I asked grimly. "I will that" he said, as he walked past me to where the insatiable cattle were now cropping on the manse lawn. "I will that" repeated Jonathan. "Of that you may be sure". Never a word of apology. Just the promise of two bags of potatoes.

Annie had been watching the whole tragi-comedy from an upstairs window, convulsed with laughter. "As you shoved these overfed beasts through the gate" she said, "I couldn't help thinking, a little irreverently perhaps, of your text last Sunday—'It is easier for a camel to go through the eye of a needle ...'" "I'm sure the pearly gates will be a little wider than mine" I replied. "Anyhow, that'll get the old codger going with the fences".

In fact, it did, but it was a miserable patchy job. "That wouldn't keep in a sheep far less a cow" I said. I didn't realise how prophetically I spoke. Only a week or so after the 'repairs' had been effected we had a spell of very hot weather. One Sunday was torrid and before we went off to Church Annie suggested we leave all the doors and windows open to give the old place a good airing. We did that and went off to the Kirk in a worshipful spirit. We had a well attended Service and Annie complimented me on my Sermon. As we walked home in the bright sunshine I was in a mood even to forgive Jonathan all his trespasses—and trespassers. The Euphoria, however, was of short duration. As we came along the manse drive I noticed that part of the 'repaired' glebe fence was down. But all Jonathan's cattle were contentedly grazing wherever they could find grass among the thistles. Suddenly I heard a scream from Annie who had preceded me into the house. "For heaven's sake" she cried "come upstairs at once". I went up three steps at a time and could hardly believe my eyes. There were several sheep on the landing and others emerging from the bedrooms. We hounded them out as quickly and humanely as we could. There was no damage done as far as we could see. I heard Annie singing a slightly altered version of the old nursery rhyme "Mary had a little lamb ... and left their trail behind them". "Thank goodness it wasn't the cows" she said as she wielded the brush and shovel. "And, by the way" she asked, "did you recognise the organ voluntary this morning?" "Can't say I did" I muttered. "Believe it or not" said Annie, "It was 'Sheep may safely graze'".

Yes, there was a funny side to it all but Jonathan must be brought to his senses, I decided. We would no longer have him as a tenant of the glebe, so that very afternoon I wrote him a letter giving him notice to quit, and sent it by "Recorded Delivery". Two days later I called a meeting of the Church court and informed them of the action I had taken. Half the office-bearers were farmers including three cronies of Jonathan. These three objected strongly. "You were a bit hasty minister, were you not. I think you should reconsider the matter" said one. "I have no intention of doing so" I replied with some heat. The matter was put to the vote and justice and commonsense prevailed. Ten supported my action, four were against. So that was the end of the Jonathan saga, and the end of a beautiful friendship. I was no longer a Christian gentleman in Jonathan's eyes, nor was Annie thereafter styled the flower of the glen. But at least, with new fencing put up around the glebe, we were safe from marauding cows and invading sheep. Jonathan never forgave me which I thought a little unfair considering how often I had forgiven him. We did meet on the road several times afterwards. He ignored me but still, head in the air, he would sing a hymn, directed to me and not to the Creator. We did not live up to the tradition of David and Jonathan.

THE BUDGERIGAR

How could I have foreseen what my first duty would entail as I sallied forth on that bright summer morning. It would be my very first visit in my new parish. As I walked along the High Street I breathed in the myriad scents of June. A willow-warbler sang, a rippling arpeggio, from the depths of a leafy beech. The sky was an incredible blue. How truly Browning wrote, I thought—"God's in His heaven—All's right with the world". And anyhow, if he was being a little optimistic, and a few things did need setting right, was I not provided to deal with any emergency, like the Knight in Alice through the Looking Glass? True, I carried no beehive or mousetrap, nor was I wearing anklets "to guard against the bites of sharks". But had I not spent four years at an ancient University, and another four at a Theological College, under the most brilliant professors? Was there any eventuality I could not deal with, any problem I would not be able to solve? Surely not. And as an extra safeguard, I carried in my capacious clerical pocket, a little Vade Mecum entitled "Prayers for all Occasions". But of course, I would never have to resort to that. No point in needlessly troubling the Diety, my being so well equipped.

Alas and alack, how little did I guess what was in store for me, quite literally round the next corner. I turned off the High Street into secluded little Abbey Lane and lifted the knocker of Number 3. Knocking on any door can be a prelude to adventure, but few of the kind I was to experience. My pastoral notebook informed me that the resident within was one Maggie Gillan aged 86. (The aged and the sick are priorities in a minister's pastoral work). No word of the lady's marital status, just Maggie Gillan. I visualised a dear old soul and anticipated an hour of gentle reminiscence, followed by a reading of Scripture and a prayer. So I was totally unprepared for the hysterical old dame who answered my knock. Straight of spine she was, not a weak vertebra. I could see at once that, like Cleopatra, she was capable of infinite variety, and that was fully confirmed in the next few years of our acquaintance. "Oh" she cried, when she saw my collar "It's the man of God himself, and ye've come in an answer to prayer. I've been asking the Lord to send somebody quickly, and He has heard my petition. But you must hurry if he's to be saved. Oh Jimmie, poor Jimmie" she moaned.

I pictured myself administering the last rites to a late repentant sinner. "What's wrong?" I asked as we went along the passage. "Is it your husband?" "Na, Na" she said "I hinna got a man, mair's the peety. It's Jimmie, my budgie, he's fallen into the traycle. Oh, hurry up, for hiven's sake, hurry". I followed her into the kitchen to deal with this unforeseen crisis, hastily turning over in my mind the pages of my book of prayers "for all occasions". But for the life of me I could not recollect seeing a prayer for a budgie immersed in treacle. Evidently the Lord was leaving me to my own resources. The kitchen table was set for a frugal meal. In the centre was a large tin of Lyle's syrup and sure enough, sinking very slowly into the sweet morass, was a little blue budgerigar. He was already up to the neck and there was a look of hopeless resignation in his tiny eyes. Clearly, although his wings were pinioned, his minute soul was on the point of taking off to the budgerigar's heaven. "A skylark wounded on the wing, Doth make a cherub cease to sing". "What was that?" asked Maggie. "Oh, just a line from William Blake, the poet", I said. "Willie Blake the grocer? I didna' ken he wrote poetry. But never mind him, save poor Jimmie" she screeched.

Heedless of the consequences to my brand new clerical garb, I put my hand deep into the syrup tin and carefully extracted Jimmie, now almost up to the eyes in the deadly nectar, at the same time bidding Maggie fetch me a basin of warm soapy water. This she did, half-sobbing the while. I transferred the glutinous birdie from the tin to the basin and laved the little morsel with extreme care, offering a silent extempore prayer, since it was the first time I had attempted this particular operation. My thoughts went back to the occasion when I ventured to bathe my own firstborn. That was true, but clearly I thought the lack of feathers on a baby does facilitate the washing process, not to mention the absence of any viscuous substance.

Throughout the long rinsing process, Maggie sat watching and moaning gently, but when the last trace of golden liquefaction had been removed from the last tiny blue feather, and Jimmie actually stood up on the table, she couldn't contain herself. "Praise the Lord" she cried. "I aye believed He answered the prayers of the righteous, and noo I ken, noo I ken". Then unbelievably from the small throat of the liberated budgie came very clearly "Kissy to Jimmie. Kissy to Jimmie". Now as this happens to be my own name I took this as an expression of thanks to his deliverer. Maggie was profuse in her gratitude. "The Lord bless you and make His face to shine upon you" she said piously. Clearly my first parish visit had been a success. I hadn't saved a soul perhaps but I had saved a song for Maggie. And no thanks to my professors who had lectured at great length on extricating sinners from the mire of wickedness, but not a word, not a single word about rescuing a poor budgerigar from the golden viscosity of Lyle's syrup.

As I left Number 3 Abbey Lane, Maggie was lisping sweet nothings to Jimmie through the bars of his cage. "Keep the lid on that tin" were my parting words. "I'll do that" she replied. "I've finished wi' traycle altogether. It's a dangerous substance. After this I'll stick to jam". An inappropriate phrase I thought, as I ruefully examined my syrupy cuff.

My first visit had occupied the time I had allowed to three, but it was time well spent. That night, however, I wrote two letters, one to my one-time professor of Practical Theology, pointing out the inadequacy of his curriculum; the other to the Church's Publications Committee suggesting that if the little book on "Prayers for all Occasions" were ever reprinted they should be honest and substitute the word "most" for "all". That night too in choosing my praise list for Sunday I decided that the opening item must be the 40th Psalm—"He took me from the fearful pit—And from the miray clay, And on a rock He set my feet—Establishing my way. He put a new song in my mouth..."

For my text I chose the words "Out of the strong came forth sweetness". Several members of the congregation remarked that I had preached very feelingly on the Sunday. One elder said "That was a grand text—out of the strong came forth sweetness, where did you say it came from in the Bible?" "From the Book of Proverbs" I told him. "That's strange" he said. "The only place I've ever seen it was on a tin of Lyle's syrup". "Yes" I said with a faint blush, "I believe I've seen it there too".

PROGENY

Don't misunderstand me. I loved my children, our children I should say. Like every other normal parent, I thought there were no children like them. That, of course, is an ambiguous phrase and it was the dubious side of the ambiguity that bothered me. I never knew what to expect, apart from the almost inevitable embarrassment, particularly in public, and in the Church of all places.

I think it is a mistake to bring children to Church at too early an age, other people's children perhaps, but not the minister's. Colin was not quite three when Annie took him to our Harvest Festival. His first Service would at least be colourful and memorable. The flowers and the fruit and the children bringing in their gifts would hold his attention and keep him quiet. And so it happened. The organ and the singing too held him in thrall. I had never known him to be silent so long. I was greatly cheered. My eyes met Annie's and we smiled. Who would have believed it of our Colin. But our mutual ocular congratulations were premature, I might have known. As soon as I began my sermon Colin lost interest. I had evidently switched him off. I was on the wrong channel. Annie decided on preventative action and surreptitiously handed him a polo, the little round sweet with the hole in the middle. "That'll keep him quiet for a bit" thought his mother. She didn't reckon with Colin. He toyed with the sweet for a moment or two, then, before Annie could stop him, he stood up on the seat (the front seat it was) and faced the crowded assembly. Then, holding the confection to his eye as if it were a telescope he looked through the hole and called out "Mummy, I see lots of people". An audible titter came from all the pews. "Come up and look Mummy" he continued, but Annie, her red cheeks redder than ever they'd been, declined the invitation. Instead she grasped her recalcitrant progeny round the knees and dexterously reseated him, despite his loud protestations. Strangely, he was quiet after that, but the damage had been done. I bravely continued with my sermon but I doubt if it made the slightest impression on the congregation. After all, you can't hope to compete with a child—playing polo.

I may say Colin did not reappear in the manse pew for another six months, by which time he was somewhat more biddable, but still unpredictable. To this day, the folk in church that Sabbath will tell you they have forgotten all about my sermon but they still remember the pleasure a little boy gave them at the Harvest Festival. Archie remarked, after that Service "What Colin said must have been very encouraging to you—'I see lots of people'—after all that's what makes a Church isn't it, lots of people?"

Mike, Colin's brother, should have known better, for he was a mature seven years of age when he blotted his copy book, (or was it mine)? Long sermons I know can be a weariness to the flesh. After sitting in a pew as a listener on a number of occasions, I am convinced that the mind can take in only what the seat can endure. On this particular Sunday Mike's fundamental durability reached a point when his mental receptivity was nil. He had had enough and made that plain to all present when in a clearly audible voice, just when I was working myself up to an impressive peroration, he called out "Oh daddy, say AMEN". I think, somehow, the effect of my peroration was lost. Never after that did I preach a sermon lasting more than fifteen minutes.

But Mike redeemed himself on another occasion, if redeemed is the right word. It happened during the great freeze-up already referred to, when every water-pipe in the village had to be dug up and replaced. And it so happened that Mike on his way home from school one day, had to jump over a deep trench not far from the manse. By then the plumber's labourer had gone home but had left his pick at the bottom of the trench. This was a temptation and an invitation to a boy of seven. He had never wielded a pick before so he thought he'd like to try it. As there was no-one in sight he slid down into the trench and, with some difficulty, tried to wield the pick as he had seen the workmen do. So engrossed was he that he was unaware of the approach of the massive figure of the local policeman. The officer had no idea who Mike was as he hadn't been in the village very long. Anyhow, here was a law-breaker, a young delinquent, a vandal, and the bobby, in what was intended to be blood-chilling tones, shouted down "Come up out of there you little devil!" Mike looked up at this insulting figure and said, indignantly, "I am not a little devil, I am the minister's son". "That put me in my place and tendered me speechless" said the policeman when later he recounted the incident to me. Well done, Mike, I thought, in declaring your status with such pride, you made me more aware of mine, and I must try to be worthy of your concept of the ministry, and remember that I am your father.

When I told Archie of the incident he chuckled and said "At least he made it quite clear to the police that he was in no way related to his satanic majesty. Which reminds me" (everything I said to Archie reminded him of something)—"which reminds me of a minister I knew who one day met the local atheist who never missed an opportunity of taunting the old man. 'Good morning Satan' he said on this occasion. The minister smiled and said 'Oh good morning my son' and passed on his way".

Children I think were born to keep us humble. We set ourselves out to teach them forgetting that we have a lot to learn from them, and at a very profound level at that. For example, one Saturday night when I was working hard at my sermon (Archie was horrified that I left it so late to prepare my Gospel message) a wonderful and humbling thing happened. Let me say in parenthesis and in defence of my late preparation that I had had a very busy week, two funerals, a wedding, a prayer-meeting, hospital visiting and so on. Archie wasn't quite satisfied "You should have your two sermons cut and dried by Friday". "Well" I said, "I usually have them cut by then". He got my point. "No offence, minister" he replied "I don't think you could ever preach a dry sermon". A great compliment that coming from Archie. But to return to that Saturday night. I was really under pressure. I had shut myself up in the study, hoping and praying no-one would interrupt me. However, just when I was getting to grips with the text I had chosen, a gentle knock came to the door. "Who is it?" I asked, somewhat sharply. "It's Margaret" said my three year old. "Please go away" I said, "Daddy is very busy". She went and I got down to my homily again. But shortly after, the knock came again "Who's there?" I asked more sharply than before. "It's Margaret", came the gentle reply. "I thought I told you I was very busy" I said "Now please don't interrupt me". What I am doing is very important". There was a brief silence, and I was sure she had gone away, but the knock came again. "Who is it now" I asked, raising my voice to show my displeasure. "It's Margaret" came the timid answer. "Didn't I tell you I was very busy and that you were not to come back?" "But daddy I have a message for you" she said. "All right" I replied. "Come in and tell me your message and then go off to bed as quickly as you can". The door opened. Unabashed and smiling she came into the study, across to my chair. She put her arms round my neck and said "Daddy, I love you", kissed me, skipped away, closed the door and left behind a very humble man, near to tears. "There was I" I told Archie later "preparing a message for my people, so busy with this important task that I almost shut out a messenger who had come directly from the Presence". "I wouldn't be surprised" said Archie "if you changed your text that night". "You're right Archie, I did. I took the verse 'Except ye become as little children you cannot enter the Kingdom' and many still recall that sermon". "I do too" said Archie "and you never preached more movingly. Now I know why. There's a lot in what the Good Book says 'And a little child shall lead them' ".

That wasn't the only time when one or other of my children determined what the theme of my sermon should be, and it never was a sermon, as some may think, on one of the "Thou shalt nots ..." One unforgettable instance comes to mind. From earliest childhood Colin had shown initiative and imagination. He was not academically inclined and paid little attention to his 'lessons', but on the last day of his first school year he came home quite excited and said proudly "Teacher says I am the best of the poor ones". This was meant to belittle Colin for, because of his pranks, he was not a favourite of this particular teacher. But Colin was not belittled; he took it as a distinction conferred on him—The *best* of the poor ones. Better, I thought, in football parlance, to be at the top of the second division than at the foot of the first. Or as an old Scottish proverb has it "Better the heid o' the commons than the tail of the gentry". My theme for Sunday's sermon came to me in a flash. Paul's claim to be "The chief of the sinners and the least of the saints".[5] But in retrospect, despite his self-devaluation, all Christendom would agree that Paul was pretty high up in the first division. And Colin has proved his satirical teacher wrong. He has made his way in the world through sheer initiative if not scholastic ability, a young man of courage and with a great capacity for caring.

O MISTRESS MINE

John Maciver was one of the most pious men I ever met, genuinely so. When he first met Annie he was the essence of highland courtesy, but he said very little, which was not like him. I suspected something, but what? On a later visit, when I was by myself, he made himself very clear. John was a great theologian and we talked at some length—and depth, on the subject of predestination. Then we went on to discuss Paul's illiberal attitude towards women. Then quite suddenly, John came out with what was on his conscience to say. He prefaced his criticism with what he intended to be an appropriate quotation from Scripture—"Faithful are the wounds of a friend". I knew then that something was coming. When it did come it shook me (inwardly) for it was totally unexpected. He continued diplomatically "I could say this much better in the Gaelic (his native tongue); its a language you can express yourself with great tenderness, without hurting a man's feelings. But since you are not fortunate enough to have the ancient tongue I must needs say what I have to say in English—a barbaric language". "That's all right John" I said with a smile. 'You won't hurt my feelings". "Good" he said "I'm glad, well then, speaking as one Christian to another, this I feel I must say—I don't think you should have married a girl that was so young, and so beautiful. It must be a terrible distraction to you, and you a good bit older than your wife". "There's only

5. Paul stresses his humility through his Letters. Ephesians 3 v.8 and Timothy 1 v.15.

ten years between us" I said and I might remind you that John Knox in his fifties married a very good looking girl of fifteen".[6] "Ochone" he said, "And I didn't think any the more of him for that". "But" I replied "It didn't hinder the progress of the Reformation in Scotland. She may have been more of an inspiration than a distraction".

"Maybe aye, and maybe no" he said, after a bit. "I never even saw a picture of the lassie, so I could not say she would have distracted him more than your wife must distract you. It's no right, and it's no wise, but (piously) I suppose it's God's will". I chuckled inwardly glad to think that in the eyes of a godly man, the Almighty saw fit to permit certain things to happen that was neither right nor wise, especially in the sphere of romantic relationships.

Annie was highly complimented when I recounted this conversation to her, remarking "Since John spoke so feelingly on the subject, might it not be possible that in his pre-conversion days, he himself was distracted in the way he thinks you must be"? "There's something in that" I said. "Anyhow, I'm glad that he conceded it must be God's will that I married you, distraction and all".

The fact of her youth, (Annie was twenty when we married) had certain disadvantages, in the early days in our first parish especially. When she answered the door, on more than one occasion a parishioner who wanted to see the minister would say quite innocently "Is your father at home"? The age gap after twenty five years, of course, is still the same, but Annie had changed remarkably little. My locks, however, once blond, have been frosted by the cold touch of time, so that my fear now is that, when she opens the door to a stranger, she will be greeted with "Is your grandfather in"? I'm sure John Knox must have suffered that indignity many times when his teenage wife answered the door of the manse of St Giles.

The "unpaid assistant" as the minister's wife has been called, does not have an easy position in the parish. She is fair game for the critics, mostly female. If she dresses well they could say "It's not quite becoming". If she doesn't, as like as not she's dowdy. Annie had no preconceived idea of what a minister's wife should be or do. There's no pre-marital training for the position. As to

6. Knox's second wife was Margaret Stewart, daughter of Lord Ochiltree. She was about 15, he was 51.

what she should wear or look like she rightly made up her own mind, with my full approval—to be her natural self and take criticism in her stride.

It never occurred to her that she would ever be in a situation where she could compromise her husband, and herself. But such a situation did arise not long after we arrived in our highland parish. She was walking along the glen road on this day when she met old Ewan Maclean, a bachelor crofter, whose ten acres abutted on the manse ground. He had never seen Annie before but had some idea of her identity. To make sure he asked her, most respectfully of course, but using the courteous language of a past generation—"Are you the minister's mistress"? Here was a predicament. What was Annie to say, "No, I am his wife"? That would have been the truth. (She was pushing a pram, by the way). But realising what was intended, and not wishing to embarrass the old man, she replied in the affirmative, blushing slightly. "I thought so" he said "You're a bonny lass". And after chatting amiably for a while he raised his bonnet and said "I hope you'll be very happy here, and I should say it makes all the difference to a minister's work when he has a good mistress, and I am sure you will be, by the looks of you". "Thank you" said Annie and she walked on meditating on her status in a highland parish. But, she thought, the language of chivalry can be embarrassing.

That same week, however, she did blot her copybook which till then did not have a single stain on it. And all because she came to the aid of a dear lady. It was the afternoon of a fine warm day and Annie, the innocent abroad, was walking along the main street, the cynosure of neighbouring eyes. Several people stopped and spoke kindly to her and wished her well. As she was passing the door of one of the hotels, the dear old lady referred to was standing on the step. She had no idea who Annie was but with a smile she said "Excuse me dear, but can you tell me who won the Derby? I have a little bet on an outsider". Annie, ignorant of important events in the great outside world, didn't even know it was Derby day. "I'm afraid I don't know" she said to the old lady, who then asked her "Would you kindly run along to Mr Simpson's, the newsagent. He's sure to know". With no other intention in her innocent heart but to accommodate the aged dame, Annie did as she was bid and came back with the desired information. "Thank you, my dear" said the octogenarian. "What a pity. It seems I've backed an also ran again. But there's always a next time". And Annie walked on her way, thinking no evil.

Now, it's all very well to help the aged, but the story got around the village very quickly. "Did you hear about the new minister's wife? She went in to Mr Simpson's shop and asked who won the Derby. And her only two weeks here. What have we let ourselves in for"? It was even suggested this was a matter for the Kirk Session. In the old days she most certainly would have had to do penance, and sit on the Sinner's stool in full view of the congregation. But it didn't come to that, although it took some time for the gossip to die down. But before long the whole village realised that they had backed a winner.

"Even if she did have a little flutter on the Derby" said Archie, "We won't hold that against her. If it comes to that, many of us do the same thing". We left it at that, Annie and I. After all they did exercise the Christian virtue of forgiveness, even if it was for a sin that was never committed.

Annie had other experiences, equally embarrassing, but that must suffice for the moment.

THE VILLAGE

The villagers were a kindly, gracious folk. They had that old world courtesy one associates with the true highlander. They were a close-knit community, by tradition and inter-marriage. Nearly everyone was related in some degree to everyone else. For that reason Archie, himself a native, warned me to be careful, to be tactful, to make general remarks about the people, but never to particularise, certainly never if I was being in the least censorious or critical. Conspiratorially he said to me, looking around to make sure no one was listening, "We are so clannish that if you were to kick one person, the whole village would limp. So watch your step young man".

Yet existing alongside the clan loyalties and the close family ties, there were divisions, not political, but religious. The village was split fifty-fifty between the Church of Scotland and the Free Church, split but without hostility. People thought their own thoughts and went their separate ways on a Sunday, but there was no apartheid. The shinty team included lads from both religious camps, and the same was true of the village council. Yet an occasional cause celebre did arouse conflicting emotions and dormant clan fires would burst into flame. I was caught up in such a situation. Indeed I was blamed for being the cause of it. It happened in this wise as the Good Book says. The Church of Scotland had two places of worship, St Jude in the centre of the village and St Anselm at the extreme east end. The latter, undoubtedly the prettier building of the two, was used only in the summer months, St Jude's during the rest of the year.

In time it became clear that the upkeep of two Churches was placing a heavy burden on the small congregation. The problem had to be faced—one Church must be closed, indeed demolished. Naturally both "Saints" had their supporters and I could foresee conflict ahead. The affair was the talk of the village. A seismograph would have given warning of an approaching earthquake; a forecast would have spoken of imminent gales. I met the advancing storm one day in the person of Amy, an elderly spinster, gaunt, sharp of tongue, uncompromising. Without preamble she said to me "If you close St Anselm's, I'll never darken the door of the Kirk again". I learned afterwards that she hadn't been to Church for thirty years, so her threat carried no weight. But it was a straw in the strong approaching wind.

Well, D-Day came and the clans (minus dirks!) met to do battle in St Anselm's which gave that old Saint a decided advantage. The match was being played on his ground. I can remember the pines swaying in the breeze outside the Church that evening, and a dark ominous storm cloud descending on the hill behind. I thought of beginning the Service with "Fight the good fight, with all thy might", but thinking that might be misinterpreted I gave out the Psalm "I joyed when to the House of God—Go up they said to me" very suitable because St Anselm's was set on high ground. I was chairman of the meeting and, I suppose, the referee—but a referee who had already made up his mind who would win the match! St Jude's must be the permanent place of worship, and pretty St Anselm's must go. It was the only sensible conclusion. But the heart has reasons that reason knows not of, and I knew that stout hearts would be up against me that evening.

But then I had Archie, a real Sir Galahad, on my side, and Ian and Donnie and a solid phalanx of sensible men. Two officials from Church headquarters in Edinburgh put their case (for St Jude's) very persuasively. But officialdom, even when it is eloquent, makes no impression on tradition. I outlined the situation and the meeting was then open for discussion. Well, the verbal battle swayed hither and thither and the outcome at one point seemed uncertain, expecially after the Colonel's speech. He was an incomer, without a drop of highland blood in his veins. He had been in the village for a mere ten years. Having come from Poona, he was accustomed to crack the whip. And now he took it upon himself to champion the cause of St Anselm's. "Watch out" whispered Archie who was sitting near me "Here comes Goliath. Have your sling ready". Well, the Colonel gave a stirring speech, worthy of a clan chief "Ladies and Gentlemen" he began "I know what a valuable part tradition plays in your lives. I know that you are a true and loyal highland people. Now, I would remind you, and the minister that the land on which this Church was built was a gift from the Laird, a godly man. Moreover, he contributed generously to its erection, and he has been open-handed in his support ever since. I am sure you are all aware of how much you owe to the Laird. And now there are those who contemplate the demolition of this beautiful santuary. What will the Laird think of such gross ingratitude? I move, with the Laird's kindness very much in mind, I move that we retain St Anselm's, and close and demolish St Jude's". He sat down amidst wide applause.

"Your sling" muttered Archie "or you're done for". I spoke as calmly as I could. "I congratulate the Colonel on his speech" I said, "I know we owe a debt of gratitude to the Laird. But you are obviously divided on this issue, so we must put it to the vote—

—Who is on the Laird's side?—(62 votes)
and—Who is on the Lord's side?—(86 votes)

It was obvious that commonsense had prevailed but for a long time afterwards the Colonel didn't look my way. He was no longer in Poona! I may say when we ultimately demolished St Anselm's we took all its stained glass windows and built them into St Jude's which is now a very attractive Church indeed, and the congregation, no doubt some regretfully, worship there in complete harmony.

I may add that after that eventful meeting I noted that the dark cloud had lifted from the ben behind the Church, and that the stars were shining with unwanted brilliance. I took this to be a sign of divine approval.

THE PULPIT

The pulpit is a terrifyingly lonely place. The minister, Sunday by Sunday, may well be six feet above contradiction, but he is exposed to several hundred pairs of penetrating eyes, and to the same number of more or less critical minds. Having produced a sermon (two each Sunday!) he must be prepared, in the northern part of the realm at least, to hear his efforts damned with faint praise. "He wasna too bad the day". "I've heard worse sermons" (that is high praise!) "Whom was he getting at this morning"? "He didn't lose much sleep over that one". "We might as well have been watching TV". These are a few of the comments a minister may expect to hear but never, of course, at first hand. The most devastating reflection on my own preaching was a discovery I made one Monday morning when I went into the Kirk to collect my gown. Passing along the pews I noticed some sheets of paper lying on the cushion of the back seat. Out of curiosity I picked them up and was chagrined to find, not appreciative notes on my sermon, but several completed games of X and O. I was cut to the quick. What price my eloquence!

The following Sunday morning, in my intimations, I told of my discovery, congratulated X of having scored more victories than O, adding, "If the contestants must amuse themselves during the sermon—'Battleships' is a much more exciting game. It requires squared paper, and if you don't know the game I'll be happy to teach you if you come along to my vestry hour". My offer was not taken up. Nevertheless, although the distance from the pulpit to the back seat is quite considerable, I saw, or imagined I did, a change in the complexion of two teenagers sitting there!

My first appearance in the pulpit was unforgettable, although I have tried to forget it. I wondered if I'd be able to open my mouth at all or if a childhood stammer would reassert itself. I recalled, but found no comfort in recalling, that John Knox, who feared no man, burst into tears and was at a loss for words, when he first went into a pulpit. I remembered too that David Livingstone, the bravest of men, was completely inhibited when he found himself facing a crowded congregation. "Friends" he stammered "I have forgotten what I was going to say". With that he turned and fled. If men of such calibre could react like that what might happen to me.

The beadle was waiting to show me to the pulpit, as the Scottish custom is. "I'm scared to death" I confided. "Och, ye'll be aricht" he said most encouragingly. "Jist keep a calm sough and preach the Gospel as best ye can. Ye canna do mair". "Thanks" I said "but pray for me". "If ye think it'll do any good, I'll certainly put up a word for ye, he said". "And look, tak this pandrop and sook it during the hymns. It'll keep your lips slockened" (moist). Well, the pulpit was at the other end of the Church from the vestry; the distance was the longest I travelled in all my life. Moreover, the pulpit was unusually high, twelve steps to glory, if I remember rightly. Somehow I got there. Somehow I got through the Service and somehow I reached the vestry without daring to look at any member of the congregation. The beadle, to my surprise, spoke appreciatively of my efforts but with this added caution—"The next time ye go up a pulpit stair, laddie, tak' one step at a time". And with a twinkle in his eye he further added, "Did ye notice that line in your last hymn 'One step enough for me'?"

With the passing of time the early terrors of the pulpit wore off, and I felt free to look around me and take note of who were present. Then I became aware of individuals and was able to spot a stranger. One bright summer morning I saw a face I felt I had seen somewhere before, I could not place it. Only afterwards I discovered it was D.H. Lawrence no less, the author of Lady Chatterly's Lover. I could hardly believe it—D.H. Lawrence worshipping in a small highland Church! Worshipping? Well he was there. I found he was on a short visit to two elderly ladies in the village who always insisted that whoever stayed with them over a weekend, no matter what their creed or lack of one, had to attend Church and sit in their pew. Which explains the presence of D.H.L. in Church that morning, conscript or volunteer? What matter, he was there.

That morning I gave a talk to the children on the theme of humility and then gave out the hymn (now happily, no longer in the hymnary) "Day by day the little daisy—looks up with its yellow eye—Never murmurs, never wishes—It were hanging up on high". I couldn't but notice the mischievous look on Lawrence's face. His gaze was directed to a large-bosomed, much bejewelled lady near by. She was singing this rather terrible hymn on humility with great gusto. The incongruity of it struck me too and I found myself smiling with D.H. Lawrence. I did not meet him unfortunately. I would have liked to hear from his own lips his comments on Christian humility!

I don't suppose people realise how much the minister can, and indeed does, see from the pulpit or they might, on occasion, be a little more discreet.

I frequently noticed that when the lights were dimmed during the sermon at the Evening Service, it was a golden opportunity for young couples in the back pews to move a little closer, and to hold hands. Why not? The time, and the place and the loved one all together? I have seen couples come within kissing distance though I have never seen osculation actually achieved. Doubtless from time to time it did happen, but who would object. Didn't Paul once write—"Greet one another with a holy kiss"? And after all it can't be very easy to give your full attention to a sermon on predestination when the girl of your heart is within whispering distance. What I do object to is people going to sleep during sermon as if the preacher were an anaesthetist. That is the ultimate insult. One man, a visitor, slumbered regularly and profoundly—fortunately, soundlessly. Yet he was always wide awake at the end of the Service. Annie, who sometimes sat beside this somnolent gentleman, told me the whole story. Not knowing who Annie was, he confided in her. "I'm staying with my old aunt—Mrs—you probably know her" he said. "If so you'll know she's strait-laced. She not only insists on my going to Church, she wants to know the text of the sermon when I return for lunch—so, perhaps you've noticed, I stay awake till the text is given out. I make a careful note of it in my diary and then I pop this little pill in my mouth—a fairly harmless tranquiliser, and I emerge from dreamland in time for the last hymn. I've timed it to perfection". Doubtless, the bedridden aunt would get the text from him later with a few original comments and, dear old thing, she would say what a good, pious nephew he was.

I can recall some embarrassing moments in the pulpit. One Sunday morning I decided to speak to the children on the loveliness of nature's music. "Why not make a recording of the dawn chorus and introduce your talk with that"? suggested Annie. "A splendid idea" I said. So, early on the Saturday morning (it was the month of May) I left my tape-recorder switched on, at the bottom of the garden, in the cleft of a rowan tree. The whole universe had burst into song and I knew I would get a good recording. I went back some twenty minutes later, retrieved the recorder and played back the tape for a full minute. The result was excellent, a joy to listen to, a concerto, arranged by the Creator Himself. "That will give pleasure to the grown-ups as well as to the children" enthused Annie. Well, at Sunday morning Service, before giving out the hymn "All things bright and beautiful" I said to the children "You are going to hear a choir singing a very lovely chorus, straight from heaven, without a discordant note, although all the singers are singing a different song". Then I switched on the recorder and the sanctuary was filled with this absolutely wonderful sound. The children were enthralled, the adults fascinated, so I thought I'd let the recording go on longer than I had intended. Then disaster struck. Suddenly into this marvellous orchestration came the hideous yowling of a cat, returning no doubt from a night out. It was as if someone had kicked a can in the middle of a Beethoven Symphony. The congregation was clearly as startled as I was. When they recovered from the shock they exploded into laughter in which I joined. I had to do some quick thinking nonetheless. "Boys and girls" I said—"there are some people who can't see or hear anything lovely without wanting to spoil it—just like that cat shrieking in the middle of the dawn chorus. That is vandalism".

And I continued in that vein for a bit hoping to redeem the situation, but I certainly did not use my tape-recorder again in the pulpit for a long time after that. "What did it sound like" I asked Annie later. With a vile pun she said "It was a catastrophe. But you did well, and turned it to good account".

Embarrassment can occur in other ways; it certainly did to me. On one occasion I was baptising several children in the presence of the congregation. Now my beadle was meticulous in the performance of his varied duties. I had never known him to slip up at a wedding, a funeral or a baptism. But on that Sunday he must have been preoccupied, hence his grave sin of omission. The baptismal Service proceeded normally. I had the first baby in my arms and had spoken the words "John Alexander I baptise you in the name of the Father and of the Son and of the Holy Spirit". Then to my horror I saw there was no water in the font. Was I to say I'm sorry, the beadle has forgotten the water" and embarrass him beyond words. Should I have whispered (he was near at hand) "Bring some water, Willie". Either way, the Service would have lost something of its dignity. So I had to think very quickly. It occurred to me, rightly or wrongly, that the granite baptismal bowl must exude some degree of moisture, however infinitesimal. The whole thing is symbolic anyhow, I reasoned. The amount of water is not important. The important thing is conveying such water (or moisture) as the font may hold and in laying the hand in blessing on the forehead of the child. So, with scarcely a pause, I went through the necessary motions. If I did wrong doubtless the Lord will forgive me. Some of my colleagues, however, may not. Anyhow there has been controversy from time to time as to the amount of water used in a baptism. Should there be total immersion, or sprinkling or just the moistening of the ministerial fingers in the font? On this occasion no water was visible. Did that make the Sacrament less effectual? One person was forever grateful that I broke the rules, if I did break them, and that was my great friend, the beadle. "I would have been mortified" he said "if you had pointed out my sin of omission". One question I always asked thereafter before a baptismal Service was "Willie, have you put water in the font"? I was taking no chances. Out of purely technical interest I have since contacted a scientific friend of mine, asking him "What is the water content of Aberdeen granite? Can it ever be said to perspire"? "Funny" he replied "I have never been asked that before".

In the pulpit of course, a minister must be on his best behaviour; he has no choice. Yet he *can* misbehave without the congregation being aware of it. In fact he can do outrageous things without being spotted, like blowing a kiss to a lady in the congregation. I should know, for I did it and not even Annie was conscious of such a gross misdemeanour. The lady in question was eighty five, the same lady as reported elsewhere, "Who won the Derby"? She was a 'character' but a most attractive one. I hadn't seen her in Church for a little time and I called to ask why. "Have you been ill"? I asked. "Not a bit of it" she replied. "I just thought I'd give organised religion a rest for a while and do some meditating at home. But don't worry,

I'm not taking up Yoga". Then, with a roguish grin, meaning to shock me perhaps, she said "Tell you what, I'll come to Church next Sunday evening and if you throw me a kiss from the pulpit, I swear I'll attend Service every Sunday. But would you dare"?

"I'd dare anything for a lady" I said. "I'll pray about it and find out from Headquarters if it can be done, and how". I didn't tell Annie about the challenge but I hated the thought of losing a regular worshipper, especially when the fee for winning a soul was so small, namely, one blown kiss albeit in public and in the sanctuary too. Well, I did pray and I believe, without being frivolous, that divine guidance was forthcoming. So the fateful Sunday Evening came and there was my old friend, tucked away in a corner seat at the back of the Kirk. Her eyesight, aided by a lorgnette was excellent and I knew she was on the lookout for the amatory gesture she had requested. She looked in vain as the Service proceeded and I was sure she thought I had taken fright, especially as I gave out the closing hymn and there was still no sign. But then came the final act of the Service, the Benediction. As I raised my right hand to give the Blessing I briefly touched my lips and described a slow gentle arc towards my friend in the corner. The deed was done. She got the message, and she kept her word. Was it then irreverence to combine the act of blessing my people with a simple gesture of love to an octogenarian, bearing in mind that the motive 'was to thirl the old lady to the Christian fellowship'.

Annie did observe the unusual motion of my right hand though she suspected no evil. "I've never seen you touch your lips before when you were giving the Blessing". "Annie" I replied, "if you had kept your eyes closed and your head reverently bowed like the rest of the congregation, you wouldn't have seen a thing". The same, of course, could have been said of my old friend but then, she had a good reason for keeping her weather eye open.

PASTORALIA

If I had any say in the training of divinity students I would include in the curriculum one or two non-academic subjects, like judo or karate, never, of course, to be used aggressively since all ministers are, or ought to be, men of peace. But in times of danger to the person they might justifiably be used in self-defence. There was the occasion for example, when the doctor told me about Alex Hollis, the butcher. "A nice, friendly, jovial chap" I said. "He's all that behind the counter" rejoined the doctor. "And at the club and on the bowling green. But at home, he is violent to a degree. And his poor wife is the victim". "I can hardly credit that" I said, "I visited them only last week and they seemed as happy as linties in the Spring. Are you sure you've got your facts right"? "Well, I treated her bruises yesterday" said the doctor. "Speak about battered wives. He'll be the death of her literally, one of these days". "But haven't you talked to him about this"? I asked. "I tried to on two occasions" he said "but he flared up and said he would allow no one to interfere in his domestic affairs. To tell you the truth, I thought he was going to attack me. And, as you know, he's a big fellow".

The news came as a real shock to me, for I had my eye on Alex for the Eldership. "Obviously" I said to the doctor "something will have to be done about it". "Aye" he said "but who's going to beard the lion in his den"? "Well I could try" I said somewhat rashly. "You won't stand a chance if he assaults you as well he might, he's six foot five and all of sixteen stone. What are you"? "Five foot nine and eleven stone" I said. "I wish you luck" said the medico. "I promise to visit you in hospital—the casualty ward". "The Lord be with you doctor" I said at parting. "He'd better be with you" he answered, smiling grimly. I was apprehensive but made up my mind to act as quickly as possible. So I phoned Hollis that very night asking if he would call at the manse the following evening, ostensibly to plan a fishing expediton on the loch—we were both keen fishers. "Delighted" he said. I wondered if he would have used that word if he had known my real motive for asking him. In case there was a scene I arranged for Annie to visit an old lady next evening. I did not explain why; I simply said I was expecting a visitor with whom I wanted to discuss a very private matter. She did look at me quizzically but if she had any suspicions she did not voice them.

Well the appointed hour arrived. Annie departed and Alex arrived shortly after, beaming and jovial as ever. I took him into the study and we sat down. I had worked out no plan of attack (or of defence). My only preparation for the interview was a prayer for guidance and, if need be, for help. I must say I would have felt safer if karate had been included in the College curriculum. Not that my faith was weak mind you. Anyhow we did discuss the fishing expedition and Alex was full of enthusiasm. "Saturday afternoon and evening any good"? I asked. "It's rather near Sunday, isn't it"? he queried. "But I expect you'll have both your sermons cut and dried before then". "I'll have them both cut anyway" I said laughing. "No offence" said Alex. "I must say I never found your sermons dry". He rose to go. "Just a minute Alex" I said. "I have a serious matter to discuss with you". "Serious" he replied, on his guard. "Yes" I said, "It's about your wife and the way you have allegedly been treating her". No time for finesse.

For a moment I thought I was for it. His face was flushed and he clenched his fists and shouted "What right have you to interfere"? "I'm not interfering" I replied "I'm intervening and there's a difference". "Did she tell you" he asked. "No" I said "she's completely loyal to you. She has never uttered a word of complaint or of criticism. Let's just say it has come to my knowledge. But I still find it hard to believe. Is the allegation well founded"? He crumpled visibly and muttered, with his head down, "I'm afraid it is". A longish silence, then, "I've been a brute without any real cause. I've got a foul temper and my wife is fair game". Then he gave in completely "I'm really ashamed of myself. But I'm relieved that you know and that you have been straight with me. I've been waiting for someone like yourself to tackle me. Before God, it will never happen again, never, never". And I knew he meant it.

He was gone by the time Annie returned. "Well" I asked "and did you have a happy visit"? "Very" she said "and did you have a successful interview"? "Very" I replied. "I was really vetting a man for the Eldership and I'm sure he'll do. "Splendid" she said, without asking who my visitor was. The fishing expedition went off as planned and we had a great time. The wind was just right, and the water. The trout didn't have a chance. We shared a basket of thirty five fish, several above a pound. I never once mentioned the interview, nor did Alex. Six months later he was ordained to the Eldership and a better Elder I never had. About that time I met the doctor. "There's a great improvement in Mrs Hollis's health" he said, smiling "and in her peace of mind too, I'm thinking. Did you by any chance do something"? "Well" I rejoined "I had Alex up for an evening and later we had a day on the loch". "Indeed" he said "so on this occasion, the big one did not get away. Good for you Isaack Walton", grinned the doctor. "You have proved yourself the 'compleat angler', a fisher of men forbye". Annie was somewhat puzzled when after the interview I discussed with her the respective merits of prayer and judo. "I'm all for prayer" she said "but judo might be handy as a second line of defence. But surely you would never use force"? "Of course not" I said "unless it were absolutely necessary".

I'm not superstitious, but it's strange how unusual things often happen in threes within a short space of time. I certainly know of no theological explanation for this. But does anything happen by chance? I wouldn't be dogmatic about it, one way or another. So I must record what happened during the week following my dramatic interview with Alex. That was on the Saturday. On the Monday morning I had a phone call from an outlying farm, some miles away. "Is that you, minister"? "Yes" I replied. "Can I help you"? "I'm awfu' sorry to trouble you" the voice went on "but the wife's very low. I dinna think she can last lang so I thought ye'd better look in past". "Who's speaking" I asked. "It's Geordie Watson o' Towheed" said the voice. "Ye ken the place, just at the fit o' the hill". "I'll come right away" I said. "Maybe there's nae jist a' that hurry" said the voice. "I'm sure she'll keep going till ye come. She's a hardy craiter". With that, Geordie rang off. "Poor Mrs Watson" said Annie when I told her of my urgent visit. "She's always been a bit fragile. You'd better go on your way as quickly as possible". But circumstances worked against me.

The old Austin, 1934 vintage, just wouldn't start. I cranked the handle, putting up a silent prayer at the same time. But neither prayer nor physical effort produced a spark of life. The engine was dead. "If you take your bike" said Annie "You could still get there in time". So I set off pedalling for all I was worth. Towhead was two miles off the traffic-beaten track and high on the hillside. With still a mile to go my front wheel punctured on a sharp stone. I had to ditch the velocipede and continue on foot. On any other occasion I would have enjoyed that walk. Broom and whin were in full bloom, their shed blossom strewing both sides of the rutted cart-track. It might have been the golden road to Samarkand, but for the sharp loose stones under my feet. A curlew rose from the hill with its beautiful burbling cry. Two oyster catchers flew stridently over my head and high in the blue an invisible lark sang praise to an unseen creator. A hare shot out from the field and stopped right in front of me, its ears erect like two exclamation marks above its startled eyes. All this I saw, and more, on the ascent to Towhead, but with poor Mrs Watson in my thoughts, I was not as joyfully aware as I might have been.

Geordie was leaning on the gate when I arrived, red in the face and perspiring freely. "It's a gey steep roadie, that" he remarked. "Did ye walk a' the wye"? I explained about the car and the bicycle and apologised for being so late. "Oh, that's aricht" he said "A body canna help these things. It's jist a' in the day's work". "And how is Mrs Watson"? I asked. "Weel" he said in a rather matter of fact tone "I thought I might manage to keep her going till ye came... But no, she was anxious to win' awa. An' she jist closed her een shortly after I phoned ye. She slippit awa wi' nae fuss, and that was it". "And what about the doctor" I asked. "Och" he said "She jist widna hear aboot sendin for the doctor. He has enough without botherin' aboot the likes o' me. I'm jist fair deen, an' that's a' aboot it. Niver mind the doctor but the minister micht come and gie me a word to help me on the road". "An that's when I phoned ye". "I'm sorry" I murmured. "Oh, thats aricht—ye couldna help it". Then, reflecting, he went on "She was aye a thoughtfu' woman. She niver liket troublin' folk an' she aye did the right thing at the right time. She was aye a good wife, considerate to the very end. Aye, she timed it weel. In fact, I would say she timed it on purpose". "How do you mean, Mr Watson"? I asked. "Well ye see" he said "She kent that we were makin' a start on the new Dutch barn next week and that it would be awkward for everybody if she was to dee then—Oh aye, she was considerate. She was a good wife, an' I'll miss her". Three days later I had a simple service in the farm-house where Jeannie Watson had slaved for forty years. Then we carried her along the golden road to her last resting place. The same lark was carolling in the heavens, a not unfitting requiem for a liberated soul.

When the phone rang two days later it was again a call to a farm, some four miles west of Towhead. "This is Willie Matheson fae Mucky Brae" said a deep voice. "Is that you minister"? "Yes" I said "Is anything wrong"? "Na, na, everything's a' richt" he said.

"The wife had a bairn early this mornin an' she would awfu' like to see you. That's if ye're nae ower busy, of course". "I'll come along in the early evening" I said. "Fine" said the farmer. "She'll be glad to see you. By the way" he added "it's a laddie, an' he's fairly makin' himsel' heard. He's got good lungs at any rate". The Austin was still hors de combat. "Something far wrong wi' the innards" the local mechanic helpfully diagnosed. But my bike was roadworthy again.

The road to Mucky Brae was little better than the track to Towhead. You had to choose your rut and stick to it for three miles. I arrived without incident and Willie met me a hundred yards from the steading beaming all over. "I'm terribly glad to see you" he said. "Come on in aboot an' hae a look at my beasties". I was surprised to say the least, but tried not to show it. For the next hour I was taken around his spacious byre, while he laid forth on the qualities of his cattle. "Grand beasts, aren't they noo" he said. "Jist look at that animal. I bocht her at the mart only last week an' I reckon I got my money's worth. Noo, ye maun come oot to the park and see what I've got there". I had no choice but to follow him and listen as he sang the praises of his Aberdeen Angus, his stots, his heifers, his bull. "I'm awfu' prood o' my new calfies" he said. Then there was the new tractor. "That cost a lot o' money" he said "but it'll dae the wark o' two Clydesdale horses". The conducted tour took a good two hours. Then, quite suddenly, he said "I'm sorry minister to tak' up so much o' your time. I'm sure ye've got much more important wark to attend to than listenin to my bletherin aboot coos. But it was very good o' you to come up a' this road, an' I hope you'll come again afare long".

I was somewhat flabbergasted. "But what about Mrs Matheson"? I asked. "What aboot her"? he replied. "Didn't you say she had a baby this morning and would like to see me"? "Losh be here" he remarked "I forgot a' aboot that. What would she say if I let you go withoot seeing' her. Come awa in, and for ony sake dinna say a word aboot my forgettin. If she kent she would say 'There's naething in his heid but beasts' ". Baby Matheson was sound asleep when I went into the bedroom. "He's just been fed" said a rosy and radiant mother. "Willie's awfu' prood o' him, aren't ye Willie"? "I am that" he said in a rather subdued tone. He saw me to the gate in the gloaming, saying pleadingly "Nae a word aboot this to onybody, minister". "I promise, Willie" I said, "see you in the Kirk on Sunday". "I promise" he said. And he was as good as his word. "Strange are the ways of Providence" I said to Annie later than night. "Not quite so strange as the ways of people" she said. I had to agree.

THE OTHER CHEEK

"If you had hit him" said Annie "do you realise you would also have hit the headlines? There would have been a first-rate scandal and you would have been out of the Church—robe, stock and cassock". "Oh yes, I know. It was a near thing. You'll admit the provocation was terrific but in the end the disciplined divine overcame the natural man". "And a good thing too" said Annie. My dear wife was never given to preaching (as I was) yet at times she could deliver a telling homily, and she was always right. "Don't forget" she would say "that these people are not just your parishioners. They are children of God and must be treated as such". "True" I would retort "but God has delinquents in His family too and, while as a Father He must love them all He must be pretty fed up with the way they keep misbehaving". "Didn't you once preach on forgiving seventy times seven"? asked Annie. "Yes" I said "but beyond the figure 490 what then"? "Come off it" said Annie "no rationalising. You know there is a divine arithmetic beyond our comprehension". Yes, Annie has thrown greater horizon round her charity than I ever did around mine.

Which is all by way of preface to telling you of a week of special temptation to violate at least one of the Ten Commandments. I leave it to the reader to judge whether I acted as a Christian minister or not. It may very well be I shall be judged by what I felt like doing rather than by my admirable restraint in the circumstances. A parish visit can unexpectedly turn out to be a confrontation. On this particular day a man in his early forties phoned and asked me to call as he had something special to say. He was not a parishioner although I had seen him in Church from time to time.

I certainly did not anticipate anything untoward and there was nothing ominous about his polite if not overly warm greeting. Now I don't know to this day what was behind the fellow's aggression. Was it an imagined slight? Did he have an antipathy to ministers in general and had made up his mind to use me as a scapegoat? Or, wishing to vent his spleen on the Almighty for His running of the cosmos, did he pick on me as His stand-in? I don't know and I never bothered to find out.

"It's a fine evening" I said by way of opening the conversation. And it was. "That may be so" was his reply "but I didn't bring you here to talk about the weather. You fellows are masters of the pleasant platitude. But I doubt if any of your parishioners, past or present, ever had the courage or the frankness to tell you what they think about you and your kind". It was a pretty fierce opening broadside, but recalling that a soft answer turneth away wrath I said "Well, I have had differences with people. I had an Elder once who frankly told me he didn't like me. I was equally frank with him and said the feeling was mutual, but could we not find a common denominator for peaceful co-existence if not for friendship? ... I can do without your friendship he replied ... He left my presence, and the Church, in high dudgeon. I regretted the incident, I must confess, for I never saw him again".

"Did he tell you why he didn't like you"? asked my teacher friend. "No" I said "I think it was simply a case of ... I do not love thee doctor Fell ... The reason why I cannot tell ... But this I know and know full well ... I do not love thee doctor Fell ..." This evoked not even the semblance of a smile from my inquisitor who, I sensed, was working himself up to something cataclysmic. I swear I heard the blood boil and bubble in his veins. And then it happened, explosively. His oaths and insults came at me like misguided missiles from the murky depths of his mind. After some minutes of this verbal cannonade I felt somewhat battered and shattered. Several times I tried to interrupt with a gentle question like "What reason have you for saying that"? But he just scythed me aside. He had a range of adjective new in my experience, blasphemy and obscenity, a sewer vocabulary. I began to wonder if the fellow was in his right mind. After all, he was an honours graduate! As the time went on I confess I felt myself grow hot under the dog-collar. Anger was building up within me. Righteous indignation, my accommodating conscience called it. Finally I fired back a salvo at him and told him, unadjectivally, of course, that he had no right to speak to me in such language.

That roused him to still further insults. "I have a right to say what I like in my own house" he shouted. And suddenly it dawned on me that he was goading me, seeking to provoke me to lay hands on him and, I can tell you, I came very near to doing it. I felt I had already turned both cheeks, several times, and was still being assaulted. There was a providential deterrent that kept me from physical retaliation. Two nights before I had opened a book called 'The Criminal Law in Scotland' and had read the section on Hamesucken. "This crime" said the writer "consists in assaulting a person in his own dwelling house. The crime has been committed even though an attempt to injure has been unsuccessful. Initially this offence was a capital one but would now be visited with penal servitude".

I was now convinced that my verbal assailant really wanted me to commit this dastardly crime. I was at least six inches taller and two stones heavier and it would have been no trouble at all to give this wretch the hiding he deserved. But, as Annie said, I would have hit the headlines harder than I would have hit him. I could see the front page of the Daily News. ... Minister found guilty of hamesucken, thrashing an innocent man in his own home ... I could see myself in the dock face to face with my cringing accuser. I could hear the magistrate say I was a disgrace to my profession. I could picture the misery of Annie at home. I could hear the schoolmaster (after hearing of my six months' sentence) saying sarcastically to my children ... "When did you last see your father"? All this flashed across the screen of my mind much more swiftly than it takes to write. It had the desired result. It was like plumping a lump of ice into a cup of hot tea. My temperature dropped immediately. It was in possession of myself and the situation. When the barrage was over and my assailant had at last run out of ammunition, I smilingly heaped coals of fire on his head (I hope) by congratulating him on the richness and extent of his vocabulary. I am sure he was disappointed. The aggressive reaction he expected did not materialise. I would not say my smile disarmed him but it obviously did surprise him. However, he had one final fling at me ... "I would say you are less than a man if you don't even attempt to defend yourself" he said. "That may be so" I replied "but in this instance at least, I have tried to be the kind of man you have so emphatically said I am not". "Well" he grunted "if you're expecting an apology you'll be disappointed. I've been wanting to get this out of my system for a long time and now I've done it".

On the wall behind him I noticed for the first time a text in gold lettering in a Victorian frame ... "Love one another" it read. He caught me smiling again and doubtless would have had something cutting to say. But at that moment the door suddenly opened and in came his wife, full of apologies. 'I'm sorry Douglas" she said. "Cousin Beatrice was not at home so I thought I'd come back and prune the roses". Douglas looked embarrassed to say the least. "But I'm delighted to see you in such good company. How good of you to call (this to me). Douglas was saying just the other day he'd love to have a talk with you. I'm sure you'll have had a very interesting conversation". "Very" I said, rising to go. "Don't go yet, please" she said. "I'll have a cup of coffee ready in a minute. Just carry on talking". There followed a rather strained silence while we waited for the coffee. Thereafter, there was no need for speech from either of us. Over the coffee she filled the silence with pleasant inanities. When I finally said I must go she observed "This will be a day for Douglas to remember. He has very few friends you know, so you must come again soon". I promised to do so with the unspoken reservation that she must be present on the next occasion.

It was a year before we made contact again. Douglas called on my services when his mother died. He made no reference to our previous encounter nor did I ... "You were the one man I thought of to help me through this crisis" he said. I thanked him for the compliment. I think divine grace, amazing grace, had been at work in his heart. In the years that followed we became good friends and he sought my advice on a number of occasions. But Annie has never forgotten the time when I came so near to ending my ministry when it had scarcely begun.

Within three days of that near fatal confrontation, believe it or not, the devil was at me again. I began to have a very real sympathy with Job and wondered if I too was being put to the test.[7] It happened that one evening I popped in to see an old lady just outside my parish. I had heard she was in poor health and miserable

7. Reference to Job. He was tried in many ways as I was!

circumstances. A brief glance at her clothing made it clear her wardrobe needed renewing. Present was a middle-aged son with all the marks of a ne'er-do-weel. But he was very obsequious and deferential. After some talk I said I would call again soon and would bring some much needed clothes for the old lady and a suit for the son. He was loud in his praise of ministers in general and of myself in particular. As it happened I was unable to lay hands on the clothes I had promised as quickly as I had hoped. I called to explain the delay. The son was slightly drunk. Seeing I was empty-handed he immediately launched an impious attack on ministers in general and on myself in particular. Not giving me a chance to explain he said "You ministers make a lot of fine promises you never mean to keep. It's all pie in the sky". There followed a verbal bombardment not unlike the one I had suffered a few days before. I was left in no doubt as to the sanguinary sort of person I was. In fact I felt there must be blood all over me. I let him go on, keeping my cool as they say. The old mother, sitting beside an out fire, was clearly embarrassed but the son disregarded her feeble protests.

At last there was a pause. "Are you finished"? I asked. "Yes" he said "and you can leave this house the way you came in". "Not yet" I said "for if you have finished, I haven't yet begun. I have something to say to you".

He looked surprised and befuddled. The worm (myself) was turning instead of squirming. "Yes" I said in a definitely non-pulpit voice "after listening to your disgusting tirade, I'll give you a choice. You'll get down on your knees right here and now and ask for forgiveness, or I'll take you into the lobby and hammer you". And this time I meant it. I wasn't in a temper. I was judicially cool and would have done a clinical job on the poor wretch. "And what happened" asked Annie. "You are not to be tried for hamesucken after all are you"? "No Annie, there's nothing to worry about. I can assure you I have never seen a repentant sinner get down on his knees more quickly". "And did he ask forgiveness"? queried Annie. "He mumbled something" I said "but I couldn't make out what it was. But I got down on my knees beside him and asked forgiveness for us both. After all I had violence in my heart and I might have hurt the fellow and upset the mother".

"Weren't you a pacifist once"? asked Annie. "Oh yes and I hope I still am. But it seems that in order to keep the peace you have to threaten sometimes to break it". "I can't quite see the logic of that" she said. "But for heaven's sake see that it doesn't happen a third time". "I promise" I said, kissing her gently on the cheek. Roguishly she turned the other saying "Isn't that according to Scripture"? We walked arm in arm through a redolence of roses in the cool of the evening. A blackbird at his vespers was singing the day to a close. Annie looked bonnier than ever. I was at peace with the world.

WEDLOCK

I would like to forget some of the things I forgot, especially that wedding. But of that, more anon. It is good for a young minister to have an older colleague as a father confessor. So, about once a month, I used to visit Dr James Allen and every visit was a tonic. Not that we always talked theology; more often we just reminisced. We had a common love for the hills; that was a topic of which we never tired. We would swap ministerial experiences and talk of embarrassing situations from which not even the Lord had been able to extricate us.

"Did you ever forget a wedding"? I asked on one visit. "Funny you should ask that" he said smiling. "One of my recurring nightmares as a young minister was that I had forgotten a wedding. I would be in the hills when suddenly I would remember the marriage service I should be performing. I could visualise the expectant congregation. I could see the nervous bridegroom standing at the altar and the divinely gowned bride coming up the aisle. I could see the alarm on the faces of the guests when the beadle announced that the minister hadn't turned up. I could imagine the bride bursting into tears, and hear cries of 'Shame' from the assembled company. Then I would waken in an agony of sweat, but greatly relieved. I had that nightmare on several occasions, with a number of variations". "Terrible", I said emphatically. "A nightmare is bad enough but it would have been a hundred times worse had it really happened I know, for it really happened to me". "Well now, that's really interesting" chuckled James. "Tell me about it". "Well" I said "I have always kept a diary, making a habit to consult it every morning, after reading a passage from the Bible. It was the 103rd Psalm—'Bless the Lord, O my Soul, and forget not all his benefits— Forget not'. Yet I forgot to look at it that day for some reason or another. It was a bright Saturday morning in May. The countryside looked lovely. Birch and larch were dressed in living green. The blackbird was shouting 'Come on out'. Forby, there was a gentle wind from the west... 'What a day for fishing'... I said to Annie. And she, as blissfully forgetful of the wedding as I was, said 'Trout for supper would be nice'. So, without more ado, I got my tackle ready, jumped on my bike and pedalled some miles to my favourite stretch on the burn. I was glad to find no-one on the water; I like being solitary when I'm fishing. Well, the conditions were excellent, but the trout did not seem to realise it". "They seldom do" interrupted James. "I remember once—but, no—you carry on".

"After a time of fruitless casting I decided to lie down in the sun, gaze up at the mackerel clouds and listen to the rippling music of the burn. Heavenly, I thought. After a time I roused myself and cast my line across the gentle current and immediately I was into a good-sized trout, over a pound I was sure. 'One for the pot, one for Annie' I thought, and then"—I paused. "Then what"? asked James. "A horrifying thought struck and stunned me like a sledge-hammer. Perhaps it was the association of ideas, but almost immediately I hooked that fish, I remembered the poor fellow who should have been hooked with my help (I glanced at my watch) some fifteen minutes earlier—The wedding. I gasped. It was no nightmare. I was fully awake. The ghastly thing had happened".

"And what about the fine trout?" asked James. "You didn't let him go, surely". "No" I said "I did not see why I should add one disaster to another. It took me only three minutes to land him, a real beauty, and I couldn't disappoint Annie".

Then, girding up my gear, and my loins, I set off like the wind. Jehu himself would have marvelled to see me go. Annie was meeting me at the door, and I wasn't sure if she was going to laugh or cry. Without preamble I said "What on earth did you do when the best man called to collect me"? "I kept cool" she replied. "I murmured something about your being called away. (I was as guilty as you were forgetting to remind you not to forget). In case my husband has been unavoidably detained, lets find out if Mr Aitken is free to take the Service".

"Old John Aitken" said James. "Of course he retired to your parish". "That's right" I rejoined. Well Annie got into the car with the best man and they drove to Mr Aitken's house. "Thank goodness he was at home" said Annie "and dressed in his canonicals, as usual. I had a whispered consultation with him and he said 'Yes, I'll be delighted'. So the long and the short of it was that he conducted the Wedding Service. I'm sure the young couple didn't mind who performed the ceremony so long as it was performed".

"You have a wife with plenty of initiative" said James. "Was there any aftermath as far as you were concerned"? "Well" I said "I discovered that the reception was being held at the bride's father's farm, some five miles away. So doffing my piscatorial togs in haste and donning my ecclesiastical attire, I cycled to the scene of rejoicing, arriving at the farm just as the meal was finished and the toasts about to begin. John Aitken made some jocular remark about the prodigal and asked me to speak first and propose a toast to the couple".

"You didn't raise your glass to the one that didn't get away"? chuckled James.

"No, no" I replied. "With an expression compacted, I hope of penitence and pleasure, I proceeded to speak of the bride's radiant beauty (a slight exaggeration) and the groom's excellent qualities and so forth and so on. And my lapse was instantly forgiven, and forgotten. It was never held against me and no-one ever asked what had detained me though some may have guessed". "It might have been very different" said James "had John Aitken not been at hand". "I shudder at the thought" I said. "Let's say that John was the Lord's agent in a crisis. The deus ex machina, the Greek dramatists would have said. But you've never said if you yourself ever forgot a wedding"?

"I was hoping you wouldn't ask that question" he replied. "As a matter of fact, I did. I was very young at the time, twenty four in fact. I had got the dates mixed up. I can't now remember why". "So it can happen to the best of men" I sympathised. "And did the bride forgive you?" 'Oh yes" said James "you see I married her". "Your own wedding"! I exclaimed. "Yes" said James "but Jane, my wife, in all the forty years of our married life, has never once mentioned it. She has a very good memory. She also has a very good forgettry! And in the event, I was only three quarters of an hour late".

Well, I learned my lesson, and I never forgot another wedding. But there were at least two occasions when I was embarrassed by someone else's lapse of memory. My organist forgot two weddings in succession, big weddings at that. He was a very conscientious chap and I was quite sure, on the first occasion, that he would turn up at the last minute. But the last minute came and went, and the bride was at the far end of the aisle, waiting to be 'played in'. I had no option but to tell the guests, some two hundred people, that the organist had been unavoidably detained. I hoped it wasn't an accident, and so on. I then said, with some trepidation (which I hoped didn't show) that I would officiate at the organ myself. What I did not tell them was, that like Robert Louis Stevenson, I could play only by ear, and that on the black notes alone. Furthermore, I did not tell them that while I knew Mendelsohn's Wedding March, I dared not play it because always, halfway through it and for some strange reason the Wedding March slipped gently into 'I'll Walk Beside You'. It had happened time and again. So, deciding not to take the risk on such an occasion, I played the simple tune 'Aurelia' set to a wedding hymn. I played it slowly as the bride with hymenal dignity came up the aisle. I then left the organ and went to the altar, welcomed the couple briefly, then with my Genevan gown flying, as someone told me later, I returned to the organ and played the opening hymn. That finished, I returned to the altar, and went through the Marriage Service. That concluded, it was back to the organ again to play the closing hymn, finally returning to the altar to pronounce the Blessing! I could not have the happy pair walk out of the Church in silence, so it was back to the organ again. All I could think of at the time was 'A Whiter Shade of Pale' and 'I'll Walk Beside You'. I chose the latter as being the more appropriate and, believe it or not, I did not put a finger wrong (or a foot, because I ignored the pedals)! Bless you R.L.S. for introducing me to the Black Notes only System.

Some guests congratulated me on my double role and I was even offered the organist's fee of two guineas! But not belonging to a musician's union I regretfully declined. At the wedding reception the best man in his speech praised me for my versatility!

I couldn't believe it when the very same thing happened at my next wedding just three weeks later—no organist! He confessed to me later that, as on the former occasion, he had gone for a walk through a field of roses and was drugged into forgetfulness of all else. I hadn't the heart to scold him. I went through the same double act as on the previous occasion, with even greater success, I think, because I had already had a dress rehearsal. But drama was unexpectedly added on this occasion, whether due to strain or to my playing, I never found out. But I had just come to the question to the groom. "Do you Ronald, take this woman to be..." when I noticed his eyes glazing and his body beginning to sway. Then suddenly, without warning, all fifteen stone of him slumped on the carpet at my feet. He was out to the world.

The congregation was naturally alarmed, many standing up. "Please be seated" I said "and keep calm". Feeling anything but calm myself, I knelt beside the fallen swain and stroked his brow and hair. In a few moments his eyes fluttered open and I whispered "I'm sure this is not the first time you've fallen for Doris (the bride) I think". He smiled, quickly recovered and stood up on his feet with some help from me and the best man. The Service was resumed where it had left off but unbelievably, just when the vows had been completed, he passed out a second time and it was almost two minutes before he came to, while I whispered encouragingly in his ear. Amazingly, the bride kept absolutely calm through the double crisis, and the service was duly completed. Once again I played 'I'll Walk Beside You' and was glad to see in the organ mirror that when the couple reached the door, he was still walking beside her. After that occasion I recorded Mendelsohn's Wedding March on tape and took it to every wedding thereafter but sadly, my organist never forgot again!

COMPROMISED

A man, they say, is known by the company he keeps. So it should have come as no surprise to me that my reputation was somewhat dented because of that early morning escapade. After all I was in the service of ONE who got himself a bad name by frequenting the company of publicans and sinners, street-walkers like Mary Magdalene and wretched little quislings like Zaccheus. Even so, it came as a shock to me when I first heard the story, told as a secret of course by one who had it as a secret, the story that I had been seen 'under the influence' by witnesses whose evidence could not be discounted. "He was wearing his dog-collar too, would you believe it". When I told Annie she laughed—"That'll teach you to keep better company and not to go stravaiging after midnight where you were almost bound to be seen".

"How do you think I could put the facts straight"? I asked. "You could include it in your pulpit intimations or slip it into your prayer of confession" she suggested. "But more seriously, forget about it. Everyone knows you are teetotal. You've made that perfectly clear at weddings and on other occasions by insisting an orangeade. And anyway, remember the motto of your university—'They say. What they say? Let them say'". Annie always had words of wisdom to impart.

The facts on which the rumour was founded should be put on record, in case anyone is not quite convinced that I was innocent of any misdemeanour at least on that occasion. And these are the facts. It was around midnight on a Saturday in April and I was working belatedly on my sermon. I'd had a busy week and now Sunday was perilously near. But thank goodness, there would be no further interruptions. Apart from the scratching of my pen, all was quiet. It was one of those nights when you could hear silence turning over in her sleep. Then suddenly the doorbell rang, shattering the stillness to fragments. "For heaven's sake" I said to myself (reverently, of course) "who on earth can be calling at this hour"? The only way to find out was to go to the door. There, very apologetically, stood a friend supporting an obviously inebriate person. 'Sorry to interrupt you at such an hour" said my friend. "But as you know, some of the organ pipes were ciphering and I was trying to put them right for tomorrow. Well, this gentleman here saw there was a light in the Church and came hammering at the door shouting 'Is the minister in? I want to see the minister'. I tried to get rid of him but he insisted on seeing you. It was a matter of life and death, he said. So here he is, I'm terribly sorry". "It's all right, Jack" I said. "Since he is in need of help, you'd better leave him here". Together we guided the fellow into my study, and Jack left, with further apologies.

I glanced ruefully at my unfinished sermon, feeling somewhat as Coleridge must have felt when he was interrupted when writing Kubla Khan; he knew the inspiration would not return. For the next half hour I listened to an incoherent story about this man's quarrel with his wife. I gathered he had quit his job, drawing out all his superannuation, and that he had drunk the lot. So now he wanted me to sort things out. But some important details were not clear. I realised that this man's case was serious, but obviously I couldn't discuss it fully until he was sober. I made very strong coffee which made little difference to his muddled mental state so I decided, perhaps unwisely, that a walk in the cooler air might have the desired effect. It was half past one on Sunday morning when we set out. A chill wind was blowing and a cold rain began to fall. "Just the thing" I thought. Arm in arm, very much arm in arm, we walked, along the street, normally quite busy but now deserted (I thought)!

My companion was a very heavy fellow and despite my attempts to steady him, we steered a very erratic course along the broad pavement. Not a soul in sight, thank goodness, I said inwardly. Then unexpectedly, from the shelter of a shopdoor, came "Ay, Ay minister—it's a chilly morning"—a bobby on his beat and, as it happened, one of my elders. "It is that John" I replied, coherently I hope. We shot away from him to the kerb and continued our serpentine course. After that, at intervals, we met three groups of young people, no doubt returning from a late party. They gave us a wide berth, but I did hear someone say "A minister, and on a Sunday morning too"!

Well, it took over an hour in the cold air and spitting rain to sober up my friend. Then, on more or less a straight course, we went back to the manse. There another hour was spent in my study, straightening the fellow out. Then promising to see him and his wife in the morning, I bade him farewell and got down to my sermon, but the inspiration just would not come. I guess it was a poor sermon, poorer than usual that is! But Christian folk are kind and forbearing, and I heard no adverse comments. Someone did say I looked tired and told me not to overwork.

How the story got about, I don't know. The policeman, to whom

I later communicated the facts, said he'd say nothing to anyone. But he may have already told his wife. Or it may be that some spy came out of the cold that momentous morning, and well, I suppose a minister is fair game. But I decided there and then, if there was any sobering up to be done, I'd do it under cover—and I would keep well away from alcohol, even when it was inside another man. I might add that on the day following the escapade, someone in the street said to Annie "Is your husband all right this morning"? "Of course" she said "Why shouldn't he be"? "Oh, I was just wondering" was the reply.

MAGGIE

My first contact with Maggie was on that unforgettable visit when I rescued Jimmie, her budgie, from a sticky end. From that day I was her friend albeit, for reasons known only to her inscrutable self, she would fall out with me from time to time. On these occasions she would say to a mutual friend "Tell him he can just stew in his own juice". But invariably she would become repentant before I was wholly stewed, and would apologise profusely for her unseemly behaviour, without ever offering an explanation.

Maggie, in appearance at least, was one of the Creator's less successful experiments, rough-hewn and angular, fashioned but never quite finished, from a blueprint away back in time. A primitive, the artists would say. She could have been a Teniel's model for one of his queens in Alice Through the Looking Glass. Yet she had some of the fearsome dignity of the dinosaur, an admirable quality we associate with primitive creatures. Had she lived in that prehistoric world (and I have a feeling she may have, in a previous incarnation) she would have had cavemen as her serfs, and a brontisaurus as a pet.

Her life during the time I knew here was a series of crises mostly imaginary or fabricated, every crisis an excuse to involve me. She was on the telephone at all hours of the day, and sometimes during the night. I know, of course, that love should suffer long (I have often preached on that text) but I had to call up all my reserves of patience and Christian love when dealing with Maggie. I wonder what St Paul would have thought of her!

She could be and often was, distracting in Church, sitting up in the gallery in my direct line of vision, munching a noisy biscuit, or extracting crunchy conversation lozenges from her spectacle case where she had cached them. Whenever unintentionally, I looked her way, she would grin and blow me a kiss. I suppose she thought she had a right to since every Sunday morning during the twenty years I knew her, she came to the vestry with a rose wrapped in moistened linen to keep it fresh. Where she got her roses in winter I shall never know. "I hope your wife realises that ours is a platonic friendship" she said to me on her eighty-fifth birthday. I may say she rumbled along the corriders of time for eleven years after that before she finally ran out of fuel (her own phrase). In a slightly mixed mechanical metaphor she said... "I don't intend to freewheel my way to the grave. I want to get there under my own steam". And my word she did! Only two days before she left the motorway for the No Through Road (her own expression) she demonstrated to me how she could still touch her toes without bending her knees. Not bad for ninety-six I thought. She had this in common with Cleopatra, that time made little impression on her outward frame, but I doubt if Anthony would have succumbed to her charms. Her face, in Sidney Smith's phrase, may have been a breach of the peace but she had an indomitable spirit. She was in some ways unmovable if not irresistible, for once she told me she had been run into from behind, by a Mercedes no less. The doctor who examined her said there were no broken bones, only a distinct imprint of the two hemispheres on that part of the anatomy specially designed for such a cartographic exercise. The mechanic who examined the Mercedes said the radiator would have to be replaced.

To my knowledge Maggie was only once ill, and that not seriously. No virus would have dared to attack her. An undiagnosed malady confined her to bed for three weeks during which period she was subject to strange delusions. People and creatures were coming out of the wall or stepping from the TV. "Can't you see these wicked things"? she would ask me. "No" I would say "but I am sure you can". One day she greeted me with "Good news. I have got rid of all those silly delusions". "Great" I said. "Yes" she continued "I was just telling the captain about it". "What captain"? I asked.

"Why, the captain of the liner moored just outside my window there".

In her will Maggie left all her money, not a few thousand, to a charity of her choice. To me she bequeathed her old wireless set which has never worked and never will, but which I still retain as a reminder of a remarkable platonic friendship. Annie has no objections though she leaves me to dust the sacred object myself.

Maggie always had the last word, save for one occasion. She stipulated in her will that no one should be present at her cremation except myself and that the Service should be as short and cheery as possible. "Dinna greet for me when I take my leave" she once said to me. "I'll feel at home where I'll be going". "And where's that" I asked. With a wink she replied "That remains to be seen, though I must say I am partial to heat".

Well, when the day came to bid her a ceremonious farewell I must say I could not suppress a smile despite the time and place. As I looked her way, regally covered by a purple catafalque, I thought to myself "I have the last word on this occasion, Maggie". But I didn't actually say it ... just in case! And so she stepped out of time into eternity, not without dignity. Whether all the trumpets sounded for her on the other side, as they did for Mr Valiant-for-Truth, I cannot tell. A roll on the celestial drums, perhaps.

In the hierarchy of the angels she may not have a very prominent place, but I wouldn't be surprised if Peter made her chatelaine of the Pearly gates. She certainly would not let anyone in without thoroughly scrutinising their credentials. She was that sort of woman was Maggie.

ANGUS

I never met anyone quite like Angus. Charm? Charisma? Magnetism? No one word would comprehend his personality. Small of stature, large of intellect, his imagination was without horizons. He spoke English with a lilt, for Gaelic was his native tongue; and, of course, the only true Gaelic was the Gaelic of the Isle of Lewis where he was born. All other branches were derivatives. And yet, he would say, even the most decadent forms of the Gaelic were preferable to the insipid tongue of the Sassenachs. Shakespeare would have been that much greater had he been born in Lewis, for then he would have written his plays in the language of Eden. "Do you really believe Adam and Eve spoke the Gaelic"? I once asked him. "Believe it"? he said, "of course I believe it. The Almighty would see to that. Only the best would do for the founders of our race".

Hebridean folk are proud of their origins, and no wonder, if what Angus told me is true. "You know, the whole story of Creation is not included in the Good Book" he said to me as we lay one day in the heather by the shore of Loch Cama, the Crooked Loch.[8] "But I will make good the omission for you. You see, the Isles of the Hebrides were an inspired afterthought of the Creator. The idea came to him as He rested on the seventh day. Looking over the high edge of heaven on the earth below He saw that it was good, very good. But to crown it all He must make something superlatively beautiful. Matching the deed to the thought he took a great handful of emeralds and amethysts and flung them into the ocean along the western seaboard of Scotland. Then, surveying the shining archipelago with pride He said to Himself... 'Yes, that's it. That's my masterpiece. Now I can rest content'. And that" said Angus "is how the Hebrides came to be". Who was I to gainsay him? He evidently had inside information to which the biblical scholars did not have access. "But" continued Angus solemnly, "the Lord made one mistake. He made the islands too beautiful, so beautiful that when the natives who departed this life arrived in heaven, they would invariably cast a backward and downward glance, with tears in their eyes, so lovely did their dear islands look from the high vantage of Paradise. And, you may not believe this, but many expressed a desire to return. Realising His mistake, the Lord made haste to rectify it, and He decreed that tenuous blue mists would hang like a veil over the islands for most of the year, so that they were but dimly visible from the celestial fields. And that put an end to the nostalgia of all the arrivals in Tir-nan-Og.[9] And of course" added Angus "since he scattered His gems from the north to the south, Lewis would be the first to settle in the ocean, the first and

8. Loch Cama near Lochinver, Sutherland.
9. Tir nan-Og. Literally land of the young.

the best and the most beautiful of them all, the very Koh-hi-Noor of the Crown Jewels of the Creator".[10] Again, as I said, not being a Lewisman and not having the Gaelic, who was I to question the veracity of such a tale, told with such conviction. "You may think I'm joking" said Angus "but some day you'll get confirmation, and you'll be remembering what I told you by the shores of Loch Cama, with the heather all in bloom".

How did I first meet this remarkable man? It was in this wise. It is the duty of every missionary on furlough to visit various parishes in Scotland (as planned by Church H.Q.) to speak about his work in the foreign field. And Angus's parish was on my itinerary. Needless to say, Annie came with me on all these occasions. On our way west one day, we drove through miles of heather-empurpled moor, past lochans that mirrored the mountains on their polished surface. Suddenly we topped a rise and got out of the car; we had to, for the panorama that met our eyes, such as silenced poor Cortez when he looked for the first time on the Pacific from a peak in Darien. Annie and I were silent too, for there, floating on the western sea, dreamlike through a thin blue haze, were the amethystine shapes Angus was later to tell us about, "The Hebrides" I cried. "No" said Annie "Fragments of Heaven" not knowing that before long Angus would verify the statement. Only when the light began to fade and the islands became indistinguishable from the sky, did we think of resuming our journey.

"Had I not better change out of these"? said Annie, indicating her trousers. "It wouldn't do to arrive at a Highland manse in such unseemly garb". "Perhaps you'd better" I said. So there, behind a knoll, far from the cynosure, or censure, of neighbouring eyes, Annie stepped out of her trouser suit into a sedate skirt and jumper, and we were on our way.

We found the manse nestling in a grove of oak trees, and the scent of bogmyrtle, as we drove along the avenue, was a foretaste of all the good things we were to enjoy in that corner of heaven for the next few days. I rang the bell with some trepidation. The door was opened by the mistress of the manse, young, slim, bright-eyed

10. Koh-hi-noor. Famous Indian diamond which became one of the British Crown Jewels on the anexation of the Punjab in 1849. Hence, anything superb of its kind.

and welcoming, and wearing?—yes, a trouser suit. "A thousand welcomes" she said in Gaelic and in English. "Come in and meet my man". And there was our first glimpse of Angus before a peat fire, his arms outstretched in greeting. "How good to see you" he said, with that lilt we learned to love. "I must say I expected to see an older couple, certainly not a bonnie young lassie like you". This to Annie. Then he said something in Gaelic to his wife which set her laughing. "What was that"? I asked. "Och" she said, tossing her head "he was just remarking that she was too good-looking to be a minister's wife". "And what about yourself" I said gallantly. "Away with you" she replied "you men are all the same, and of all men you ministers are the worst". Such was our first encounter with Angus and his good lady, and it was the beginning of a long and splendid friendship which will be continued across the borders of time into the land of Tir-non-Og whither Angus has now gone.

Angus had two great passions, he was a fisher of salmon and of men (in reverse order) and he was an expert in both of these arts. "After all" he would say "these were Peter's two occupations. They are not mutually exclusive as some may think. While fishing quietly on the loch or the river I'll be thinking deep thoughts and working out my sermon for Sunday. There have been times" he added "when not wilfully mind you, I have broken the commandment with regard to the Sabbath, but it was in a good cause, you understand". "Tell me" I said, as we sat in his study surrounded by learned theologians safely imprisoned in leather-bound volumes, "Did I spy Isaac Walton amongst them"? "Well" he began with a slow smile, "one Saturday evening I could find no inspiration for the sermon and the time was wearing on. It was eleven p.m. in fact. Och, I said to myself, I'll just go down to the river for a cast or two and maybe in the quietness some bright idea will come. And sure enough it did. The river was my friend. I had the whole sermon worked out when, at ten minutes to midnight, my very last cast, I was into a big fellow who ran away with half my line. I knew I was in for a fight and the Sabbath now less than ten minutes away. I was tempted to turn back my watch. But that wouldn't be ethical. So I argued in my mind ... is it the greater sin to nibble just a little bit off the Sabbath or let this fine fish go? I wasn't at all sure so I said a little prayer for forgiveness to be on the safe side, keeping a tight line all the time. And at last, fifteen minutes into the Lord's

Day, eighteen pounds of gleaming silver lay on the bank at my feet. What a beauty. Now what do you think of that, brother, the ethics of it I mean"? "Well" I replied "I think Peter would have said your watch was a bit fast, say fifteen minutes". "That's the way I looked at it too" agreed Angus. "But now I was faced with a fearful dilemma, I might be discovered. You see, I had to walk the whole length of the village street to get to the manse... And it was mid June with still plenty light, and there would still be folk about". "So what did you do to avoid scandal"? I asked. "Well, like a naughty boy, I hid my rod and tackle in the long grass and then I contrived to get the salmon down my trouser leg so that, with my hand in my pocket, I could hold him by the gills. And I can tell you that cold salmon next to your skin doesn't raise your temperature even on a June night. Well then, I walked peacefully and sedately home, the whole length of the street" adding with a note of disappointment after all the trouble he had been at ... "and do you know, I never met a single soul".

Highlanders, generally speaking, have very high ethical standards, with certain reservations. Since the earth is the Lord's and the fulness thereof, there's no great sin, if indeed it be a sin at all, in taking the occasional stag from the hill or the antrin salmon from the river. Angus subscribed to this code and did not think that Gabriel would hold it against him on the day of reckoning. But he took reasonable precautions nonetheless. There was the evening we planned to go on the river, for example. "First of all I'll give a ring to one of the bailiffs who is a friend of mine. He looks after the lower beat where we'll be going". He duly rang up the gentleman and there followed a conversation in Gaelic, of which I understood only one word 'agus' ... meaning ... 'and'. That set a definite limit to my understanding of what was happening. But when Angus at last rang off, there was a satisfied smile on his face. "It's alright" he said "we'll be safe enough to use the garden rambler this evening. My friend Alistair says the other bailiff is off to see his cousin this evening". "The garden rambler"? I said some-what puzzled. "I thought I knew most of the salmon flies but that's a new one to me". In conspiratorial tones Angus whispered "The garden rambler is a worm, man. It's forbidden on this stretch of the river. It's too deadly. Mind you, I don't use it very often. It's not fair to the fish, or the laird".

And sure enough, we had four fish that night. I had one, Angus three, all around the nine pound mark. And whom should we meet on the way home but the other bailiff. He admired our catch. "Yes, you've had a good night of it minister. Could I ask what fly you were using"? "Now" said Angus smiling "that would be telling, wouldn't it"? quickly adding "how did you find your cousin"? 'He's very well" was the reply "but how did you know I was seeing my cousin"? Quick as a flash Angus said "I just jaloused it because of the airt you came from". "You're a clever man minister, as well as a good fisher" said the bailiff. "Well, I hope you enjoy your fish. Oich-y bha". "Do you think he knew"? I asked when our friend was out of earshot. "He might have guessed" said Angus "but guessing and knowing are two different things". To my shame be it said, I greatly enjoyed my poached salmon.

There were some three hundred lochs in Angus's parish and he had the right to fish every one of them; and I doubt if he left any of them unfished. For that matter he had climbed most of the mountains, some over three thousand feet, which ringed his domain. One day he was fishing on a very remote hill loch when he was approached by a big florid faced fellow in tweeds. "He came striding swiftly towards me" said Angus "and there was anger in his stride. I recognised him as the new tenant who had only recently taken over the fishing rights of the estate. He had no idea who I was for I was not wearing my dog collar. With less finesse than a wild bull and with no regard for the sacred silence of the hill he came up to me and shouted 'Do you know you are fishing on my water'? From my five feet five I looked up at his six feet four and shouted as loudly as he had done 'Do you know you are standing in my parish' "? For a moment he looked astonished and then to his credit burst into hearty laughter. "Well spoken padre" he said clapping me on the shoulder. "I had no idea who you were... And that" said Angus "was the beginning of a very good friendship".

The better I got to know Angus, the more I became amazed at the variety of his gifts, the outreach of his mind, the upreach of his spirit. I had been foolish to hint one evening, just to hint mind you, that perhaps he could find wider scope for his talents in some place not quite so remote from the rest of the world. "Remote", he said, his eyes flashing. "What do you mean by remote? You are as bad as these fellows from the BBC". Realising I had trodden on a sensitive area, I stammered "I didn't mean to be offensive Angus. But what about the BBC"? "Well" he said "two of them were here on holiday some years ago. Maybe they were snooping. You can never tell with the media. Anyhow they got talking to me and one of them said 'How does it feel to be so far away from the centre of things'? That made my blood boil. Far away from the centre of things, I hissed. This *is* the centre of things. It took them some time to realise that I meant it, but when they did, believe it or not, they devised a radio programme called 'The Centre of Things', featuring my parish and involving a gamekeeper, the postmaster and a few more locals. I think I got them to see things in their proper perspective. So now they know that as far as we up here are concerned, it's these London folk who are far away from the centre of things". "I'm sorry old man" I said "I should have known better". Angus spent his whole life in that parish, fishing its lochs and rivers, tramping its heather-clad moors, loving and caring for his people and greatly beloved by them all. I wonder if sometimes from his new elevation, he peers through the blue celestial veil in the hope of catching a glimpse of the amethyst that is Lewis, or of his own one time parish on the mainland just across the shining stretch of water that separates God's inspired afterthought from the rest of creation? I wonder.

RADIO-ACTIVE

"I breathed a song into the air. It fell to earth I know not where. For who has sight as keen and strong. That it can follow the flight of song". So wrote Longfellow. But he goes on to say "The song from beginning to end, I found again in the heart of a friend".

This is true of the words we broadcast (and I am thinking especially of religious broadcasts). We know nothing at the time of the 'flight' of our broadcast, but from hundreds of letters we discover that our words have alighted in a heart here and a home there, all over the world, thousands of miles from the 'launching pad'. There is a passage in the Bible that says when God's word is sent out, broadcast if you like, it does not fade out in untenanted air; it falls like seed on good ground and bears fruit. This has certainly been my experience after many years of broadcasting.

A scientist once said he never switched on his radio without first going on his knees so moved was he by the miracle of broadcasting. I too, have never ceased to wonder. My very first broadcast was during the war. It was merely a talk about religion in the Army, after the nine o'clock news. Our first-born was at home, miles away. I suggested to his mother that she should keep him up on the night to see if he should respond to my voice. He was only two and hadn't seen much of me. "Well" said Annie afterwards "he was playing with his toys, naturally paying no attention to the news; but at the first few words you spoke he said 'Daddy'. He dropped his toys, looked all round the room and even under the table for the invisible father". Now, I have found when the Word of God is broadcast, it is recognised by many of his children as their invisible Father's voice, and that they respond in remarkable ways.

I am not concerned with the technicalities of broadcasting. only with the results that come to the notice of the religious broadcaster. My very first Service, broadcast from a little Highland Church had, with many moving responses, one amusing consequence for myself. I should explain that on the minimum salary, I frequently had a small overdraft. At this particular time it was twenty pounds, a daunting figure for me. We had had a worrying holiday, due to the illness of one of the children. Annie was exhausted, and I promised her a few days at Christmas. However, the news of the overdraft washed that out. Then, a week after the broadcast, as I walked up the glen, a stranger stopped his car beside me and seeing my dog collar he said "Are you the chap that broadcast from here the other Sunday"? "Yes" I said with a smile. "Well" he said "you don't know me and anyway I'm just acting for two old friends who were greatly helped by the Service. They asked me to give you this". And he put in my hand something I'd never handled before, a twenty pound note. "Thank you" I said "did they say which of the Church funds it was for"? "Actually" he replied "they said this was to give your wife and children a holiday, if you have a wife and children". With that he smilingly drove away and left me wondering how the Lord had squared my overdraft—exactly, and made the Christmas holiday possible after all.

Now, it is worthy of note that in a single broadcast, on radio or

TV, a minister will reach more people than Jesus and Paul together would have reached in their combined lifetime. In the Parable of the Sower, Jesus says "The field is the world".[11] This is true for the broadcaster. What an opportunity, what a challenge, what a responsibility for him.

Let it be known that part of a religious broadcaster's commitment is that he must reply to every letter he receives whether it is a word of thanks or of criticism, or a cry for help. While this means a great extension of one's ministry (just as correspondence was of Paul's) it is very time-consuming. For example, after four brief Services on the Light Programme, I received some seven hundred letters. All these had to be answered, some at length and in depth, and over a period. This called for several months of correspondence. A costly exercise, you may say. Yes, but richly rewarding in the human contacts made, and the opportunity to help people who otherwise might not have found the help they sought.

Where then, as revealed by letters, does the seed of the Word fall, and what does it accomplish? It falls, as I have already said, in the hearts and homes of people of all ages and professions, doctors, teachers, housewives, servant girls, people listening in their cars, in lighthouses, in ships at sea. Letters came even from Cabinet Ministers and titled folk. The fact is that many will confide in a stranger, rather than in someone who knows them. In many cases I have found that the Word comes to people in a time of crisis and speaks directly to a given situation. Folk are comforted, encouraged, and challenged. Letters, apart from a few critical ones, are not just 'Thank you for a nice Service' but to express gratitude to God for a message that came at a time of very special need.

It is not always the sermon that strikes a chord. Quite often it is a hymn or a prayer. I shall never forget the letter from a poor woman in a London slum. I had prayed for those who felt forsaken. "I am one of those" said this writer. "In the evening of life, one looks for a little peace. I am faced with starvation, rags and eviction. Even God has abandoned me". When I read this letter from the pulpit (without, of course, disclosing the writer's identity quite a large sum of money was handed to me without my asking for it, and this I sent to the woman. Back it came by return post with an

11. Parable of the Sower. Matthew, chap. 13.

even more bitter letter than the first saying "It's not money I need ...". At my request, a little later, one of my members on a trip to London went to see this poor soul. She found her in a bad way, and utterly friendless. My member immediately took her back to her own home for a three months' holiday. The result? A completely changed life, because someone cared. God had not forgotten her after all.

On many occasions the Word comes to people who are really desperate. One young woman wrote after a broadcast. "My fiance died tragically last week, and this morning I decided I couldn't go on living. I switched on my wireless vainly hoping for some word that would prevent me from doing the terrible thing I intended to do. Thank God, the word was given. The loneliness still has to be faced but now I feel I can face it with courage. Thank you".

Naturally, the broadcaster cannot go personally to the aid of people hundreds of miles away, but he can be a bridge-builder by contacting someone near at hand and in a position to be of service. This in many cases has worked wonders in the formation of new and transforming friendships.

Letters from old folk are particularly touching. Here is an extract from a letter laboriously written with the aid of a magnifying glass, "I am grateful for today's broadcast. I am nearly ninety, practically deaf and blind. I sit close by my wireless and turn it up loud. Sometimes I switch off halfway through a Service especially when the sermon is pitching in to me for not coming to Church. I am so alone since my husband died that I could not go on but for the sense of a divine Presence and the promises of the Lord".

Moving letters come from people in great sorrow asking to be remembered in prayer, like this from a stricken father. "Last week, on a beautiful Spring day, with lambs gambolling in the nearby fields, we laid our beloved little son to rest. He was only ten and so full of bright promise. His mother and I are heartbroken, but the Word that came to us today across the air, has given us new hope and courage". Thus, an ordinary minister with no special talents or gifts, is used by God to help people totally unknown to him.

I never cease to wonder at the way the broadcast Word brings healing and cheer to so many unseen listeners. A young woman living alone wrote "Pain is my constant companion. The Service came to me today like the music of the Fifth Symphony, and God was very near.

Not a few letters are anonymous like the following—"This comes from an old couple living high up on a Welsh mountainside, to give thanks for the blessing that came to us over our small portable wireless set. Life is hard here but we have much to be thankful for as we move toward the end of the road". No self pity there, only courage and dignity and a thankful heart.

Letters came too, from people at work. The kitchen staff in an institution wrote "We had such strength, help and joy in sharing your fellowship today". And this from a teenage girl "I shall always be grateful that I switched on my wireless today. The Word I needed came to me at a time of great temptation".

The seed can fall in most unexpected places. I once heard from a convict in prison. The message had touched a hidden chord. The gist of the letter was "I believe, Help thou mine unbelief". I replied at some length seeking to help him, and he replied saying "Thank you, padre, I see life now in a different light" adding "and I will have seven more years here to think about it all". Stone walls do not a prison make, certainly not as far as the broadcast Word is concerned. It can set the prisoner free before his time is up.

Occasionally one can personally answer an SOS. I had just got into bed about midnight after a late TV Epilogue, when the phone rang. "Are you the chap that broadcast an hour or so ago"? asked a deep voice. "Yes" I said. "Could you come and see me"? continued the voice. "Certainly" I replied "I'll come along tomorrow night". (He had given an address several miles away). "If you want to save a soul you'll come now" said the voice. I dressed at once and went to the address given. There I spent some four hours counselling a man who had a problem he couldn't solve alone. That was only the beginning. Further calls were necessary but, in the end, my new found friend triumphed. It is humbling and uplifting to find that God can use one's ordinariness to do extraordinary things.

It is particularly thrilling to broadcast overseas and to receive letters from all parts of the globe. A heartening letter like this came from a lonely place in Africa. "As an exiled Scot let me say how much such a Service means to us here. The old Psalms and Paraphrases brought us into the fellowship of the folk worshipping at home. Our only child is only eight months old. You can be sure he'll be brought up in the faith and nourished by the Word".

From South America there came a letter from a lad I hadn't seen for years. He had been far up the Amazon on some sort of survey and had switched on his wireless to listen as he drank his flask of coffee. "I immediately recognised your voice" he wrote "and although the words you spoke brought tears to my eyes, they also brought joy and comfort to my heart in this lonely, God forsaken place".

One overseas broadcast was memorable because of a gate-crashing soloist. I was conducting a children's Service from the Scottish Highlands. It is quite a common practice to put "a bell microphone" outside the Church to pick up and broadcast the sounds of home for the exiles, the bleating of lambs, the barking of dogs, the sound of a train. By some oversight, it appeared the engineer concerned forgot to switch off this microphone when the Service began. The result was that a number of people from South America wrote to say, that while they had greatly enjoyed the children's voices, they were particularly delighted with the soloist. The soloist was a blackbird perched near the outside mike and every time the children sang, he too burst into song. it was lovely to think of a highland blackbird being heard all over the Western hemisphere, probably his first, and only broadcast. I have received letters from ships in mid-ocean, letters from Australia and New Zealand, inviting me out for a holiday, but forgetting to enclose the fare. A letter from South Africa from a chap who said—"I think you played outside right in the team in which I was centre half". And I was the chap.

I have said nothing about letters from scoffers and unbelievers, but these prove that the broadcast Word touches the conscience as well as the heart. I guessed that such letters were really a cry for help. Certainly they give the broadcaster an opportunity to write and state the faith more fully, and to commend Christ to His critics. I may say that, more than once, this has resulted in a change of heart.

And so, after many years of broadcasting I have discovered there is a widespread hunger for the Word of God, that many people are unbelievably lonely, and that ordinary folk have an amazing capacity for courage. I have found that as Christ healed people at a distance while He was on this earth, His word today can still do the same through broadcasting. It has been for me an honour and a privilege to have been used to carry on His healing ministry in this way.

INCREDIBLE

If you are not prepared to believe the unbelievable I suggest you skip this chapter. I certainly would not have believed it either had I not been personally involved. When I first told the story to Annie, her reaction was "If ever you write a book don't include that, at least not as fact. It's so incredible a story, especially its denouement, that people will doubt the veracity of anything else you may write. It's extending the limits of coincidence a bit too far, even in such an unpredictable world as ours". "But Annie" I said "the thing actually happened. It is *true*". "Of course it's true" she replied "but you'll have some difficulty in making it sound true".

I know that imagination can play tricks with memory, but here are the facts without frills. It all came about as the result of a broadcast. All my working life I've had a love affair with mountains. I had been a climber and hillwalker since my early youth. I had been padre to a ski battalion during the war. Ski-ing, writing poetry on the virgin manuscript of the snow, was and still is my favourite pastime, albeit I now ski more often over the mountains of memory than down the hills of reality. Like Sir John Reith I can say with some truth that I worked out my philosophy on the slopes and high ridges of the Cairngorms. I love writing about the hills in verse or prose, recapturing the joys of unforgettable days in the high inviolate places, alone, or with a friend, or with a company of Jocks in battle dress. So I welcomed an invitation from the BBC to write and present for TV a programme with the suggested title of "God and the Hills". Two months from the time of asking, the programme was broadcast and I loved doing it. Judging by the number of letters I received, it evidently gave pleasure to a wide circle of hill lovers. But the letter on which my veracity may be suspect, came from an old lady asking if I could pay her a visit. When a week later I did go to see her I was very graciously received, in the top flat of a tenement, by a charming and gentle lady in her Dresden eighties, still fair of face and clear of eye. Over tea, daintily served in old

Spode, she explained her request for my visit. "I did appreciate the broadcast" she said. "I too loved the hills when I was young. I've been through the Larig Ghru and have stood on the tops of all the hills you mentioned. And I climbed them over again with you. But there's something special I want to tell you if you can spare the time". "The afternoon is all yours" I said with a smile. "Well" she continued "the programme brought back very happy memories of my dear daughter Elizabeth. She too was a mountain lover, and was in her element on the high tops, summer or winter. She used to say she only began to come alive at over three thousand feet". "I understand the feeling" I remarked. "Well" she went on "Elizabeth had climbed all the Munros (all mountains in Scotland over 3000 feet) by the time she was twenty two. And she had a very special love for Monadh Mhor, rather a remote mountain, I believe. Perhaps you know it"? "Indeed" I said "I spent the whole of a bright Spring day, early in May it was, ski-ing down its shining slopes. A dream mountain for the skier when the snow is right, but not easily reached". "Well" continued the gentle voice "for reasons of her own, Elizabeth loved it and must have climbed it at least six times, with one or two equally enthusiastic friends. Now she not only fell in love with the mountain, she also fell in love with Eric, a young advocate who had been in her group several times. The inevitable happened, they got married. And would you believe it, they spent a fourteen day honeymoon, tent and all, tramping over the Cairngorms. 'It was heavenly, Elizabeth told me afterward'. 'I can't imagine Paradise has anything better to offer'... Just look on the wall behind you". I turned and there, just above my head, was the photograph of a lovely smiling girl, standing by a mountain cairn. It bore the motto "The summit of happiness". "Yes" said the dear lady "that's Elizabeth on her dream mountain. Eric took that on their honeymoon". I felt deeply touched, sensing sadness to come.

"Well now", she went on "in due time they had twin sons, Alastair and Ian, fine laddies. While they were still tiny they were introduced to the hills, carried on the backs of their parents, in Everest rucksacks I think you call them. Then, as the boys grew up, they made a climbing foursome, and on the boys' fourteenth birthday, they all stood on top of the mountain that first brought their parents together, Monadh Mhor; and there for the first time, they told their sons the story of their courtship and how much that mountain meant to them. The boys were thrilled and secretly resolved that some day they would make a pilgrimage of their own to this remote sanctuary which, indirectly, was responsible for their very existence. Yes, they were a happy family, loving life and the hills in particular. And then, how does one of our poets put it... I may not quote correctly... "Just when we feel safest, there's a sunset touch..." There were tears in her eyes at this point. "But am I boring you with this rather long story"? "Certainly not" I replied. "You fascinate me".

I had no idea of what was to come, though there were undertones of sadness in her voice now. "Have another piece of shortbread" she said "and drink up your tea before it gets cold". "You made me forget about my tea" I said smiling. "I'm sorry" she said. "Well, to continue, everything was fine until one day Elizabeth, who had always been a strong, healthy girl, became ill. They put off calling the doctor for a time, thinking she'd soon be alright again. 'It's just tiredness' she said. 'It'll soon pass'. But when the doctor finally did call he diagnosed leukemia of a very virulent kind. Elizabeth was a realist and insisted on being told what was wrong. She took the news with philosophic calm although Eric was shattered and the boys were terribly upset".

At this point the phone rang in the next room and my hostess rose to answer it. She was back in five minutes her eyes shining. "That was Alastair ringing me from Vancouver. He is a doctor there, and this is my birthday". "Many happy returns" I said. "Thank you" she replied. "I can't expect many more. I'm 87, you know! But where was I? Oh yes, well, Elizabeth went down very rapidly. Then one evening as Eric sat at her bedside, she said to him with a brave smile 'Time is getting short dear, and I've been thinking about things. I wonder if you'd promise me something if it's not too much bother'? 'Anything at all dearest, if it's within my power'. 'Well' she said, 'I hope you don't think I'm being too fanciful but, when the time comes, I'd like to be cremated and if you could possibly do it, I should love if you could scatter my ashes on the top of Monadh Mhor. It seems a lot to ask but it would make me very happy'. Eric's heart was very full and he found speech difficult. He kissed her on the brow and whispered 'I promise' ".

"Inevitably the time came" the narrator went on "and the day arrived when Eric set off on his far journey, alone, carrying a little oaken casket. it was a lovely summer's day, such a day as they had often shared on the blue rim of the world. On the long approach to the mountain, Eric told me, 'I didn't meet a single soul. I didn't expect to and I hoped I wouldn't. On that day of all days I wanted to have the mountain to ourselves. I had refused even to let the boys with me. So you can imagine my dismay when, topping the ridge only a few hundred yards from the summit, I saw three figures silhouetted against the clear sky, standing by the cairn. Angry as I was at this eventuality (what right had anyone to be there on that day)? I continued on my way. I had no choice for I had a tryst to keep'..." "I can well imagine how Eric felt" I said. "It must have been devastating for him". "Indeed it was" she said. "But just listen to what followed, as Eric told it to me... 'When I was about fifty yards from the summit, unbelievably I heard someone calling me by name, and one of the three came toward me crying delightedly... Fancy meeting you here! But what brings you to Monadh Mhor alone? Where is your lass?... At that moment he spotted the little casket and knew, without asking further... I cannot tell you how grieved I am, he said... But who was it Eric? I asked. 'You may not believe it, but it was Alan Kindness who married us sixteen years ago'. But I thought he was in a Church in Ottawa, I exclaimed. 'True' said Eric 'but he had come across for a few weeks holiday and had planned to visit us in ten days. He of course hadn't heard about Elizabeth. But that's not all, mother, Ian Gordon was with him'. You don't mean Ian who was your best man and who also went to Canada? I asked. 'Yes' he said 'The same Ian and very little changed. So there we were together again after sixteen years, the minister, the groom, the bride and the best man, in very different circumstances. Only this time Alan conducted a very different kind of Service on that remote and blessed hilltop, very simple and very moving, I couldn't help thinking Elizabeth would have loved it. Or should I have used the present tense, for she was very much there'..." "What a strange coincidence" I said. "...'But was it coincidence' Eric said. 'It seemed ordained that Alan should be there and somehow fitting that our best man should be there too. I experienced a strange sort of happiness in that peaceful place. I shall never forget how a lark soared singing into the blue as Alan spoke the blessing. Is it fanciful to imagine that was the spirit of

Elizabeth, liberated from the bonds of earth, happy as she always was on the heights'? That then" said the old lady now smiling through her tears, "is the story I wanted to tell you. I've never told it to anyone else but your broadcast touched a chord. Look now, you haven't touched your tea. Let me bring you another cup". "Please don't trouble" I replied. "But what shall I say? I have never heard a stranger or more moving story and I feel greatly privileged to have heard it". "I'm sure Eric wouldn't have minded my telling you" she said. "Wouldn't have"? I queried. "Why the past tense"? "Well" she said "he fell climbing alone on Ben Nevis two years ago and you won't be surprised to know that his ashes now mingle with Elizabeth's on Monadh Mhor. Only the boys were present on that occasion. And strange as it may seem, although Eric had never mentioned the incident of the lark to the lads, they both told me as they stood there in the silence, a lark high above the summit sang as they had never heard a lark sing before... Now thank you for listening" said this gentle creature. "I have found a measure of peace in unburdening my heart to you. Please come again sometime and we'll talk of other hills we both have climbed". I left her gracious presence a very thoughtful man. Are there limits to credibility, I asked myself. Well, that is not the end of the story though perhaps it should be. "That is the only part of the story people are likely to believe" said Annie, "since the old lady was obviously in her right mind and telling the truth. But it's the credibility of the denouement that will be doubted. People will say you invented a dramatic ending to convince them that truth is stranger than fiction". "Let them say what they will" I replied. "I care not".

Well it happened that some months after the interview I have described, I was returning from a somewhat boring ecclesiastical meeting in Edinburgh, comfortably ensconced in the corner seat of a railway carriage (third class). Three other gentlemen, all unknown to me, occupied the other corners. We all sat incommunicado behind our favourite newspapers. It's going to be a tiresome journey I thought. Suddenly one of my companions, breaking the silence, said "Nothing exciting in the news is there? What about passing the time gentlemen, each relating the strangest experience he has ever had, something which may seem to pass the bounds of credibility but which he can vouch for as absolutely true"? We all agreed and soon we were conversing with a friendliness which the atmosphere of a railway carriage too seldom generates. Two of my fellow travellers, both excellent raconteurs told remarkable stories, vouching for their truthfulness. The other, a quiet man sitting diagonally opposite me, said "I have nothing to compare with the stories I have heard, so you must excuse me". We excused him the more readily as he had a stammer and was very conscious of it. So now it was my turn.

The tale I have told you was still very fresh in my mind, and I told it with graphic detail as the train thundered north through the November night. There was silence when I finished and the two men, whose stories had bordered on the fantastic, agreed that mine be awarded the prize. What do you think? they asked the quiet man. "I agree" he said. For a time thereafter we were all silent. The only sound was the rhythmic clacking of the wheels on the railway line. Then suddenly the quiet man spoke, slowly and deliberately, mastering his stammer. Looking at me he said "I think you omitted to tell us one thing in your remarkable story. You said that when Eric arrived at the summit of the mountain, he saw three men, the minister and the best man and a third whose identity you did not reveal". "That's true" I said. "No mention was made of who he was, so I can't help you there". "Then" said the quiet man with a slow smile "Would it surprise you to know that I was the third man"? And indeed he was. A friend of the minister, he had climbed Monadh Mhor with him for the first time that day. He had listened to me tell the whole story without interrupting. Then came his dramatic accouncement... "I was the third man".

Now you will understand why Annie thought the story might be dismissed as something imagined. But doubt it if you must, it is true. After all, I am called to preach the Gospel and proverbially, truth *is* stranger than fiction.

PADRE

After the battle of Marengo, Napoleon issued a medal to every man who took part. On one side of the medal was the head of Napoleon; and on the obverse side the words 'Marengo, I was there'.

I have four such medals which I once dared to show on a TV programme, very briefly, and worn on the *inside* of my jacket! Why? Because not one of them was awarded for gallantry. They were medals handed out with the rations, a proof that I did take part in the war, proof that I was there. One of my grandsons has these medals now and, looking at them in the years to come he'll be able to say "Maybe he wasn't a hero, but at least he was there"!

Yes, I was there as a padre (fourth class, because presumably there was no fifth class)! At the outbreak of the war I was a pacifist and might have remained so. But after Dunkirk several hundreds of the survivors came and encamped round our village. A dozen were billeted in our manse. As I talked to these lads who had been through the fire, my views changed. I came to realise that if I was to have a relevant message for the men who came back at the war's end, I would have to be with them, sharing the same dangers and discomforts. Otherwise they might well ask, "Were you there? If not, why not"? So I decided to volunteer as a padre.

Having salt water in my blood (I came of a line of seafaring men) I naturally wanted to join the navy. In that case, I was told, I would spend the war years in a naval barracks and would never be afloat. That did not appeal to me so I opted for the Army, and served briefly with Searchlight Units and Combined Operations. While with the latter I did have contacts with the sea. I took "divisions" on the square every morning with naval personnel and was frequently at sea in assault boats and tank-landing craft. This I greatly enjoyed, but as soon as I discovered the existence of a mountain division, I asked for a transfer, hill-walking, climbing and ski-ing being my chief pastimes. Here was a chance to combine pleasure with duty, I thought! Little did I realise what I was letting myself in for. Yet I would make the same choice again.

My first attachment was to a Highland Battalion, a splendid bunch of lads. The training proved exacting. Almost immediately I found myself taking part in a rigorous divisional exercise named 'Goliath' in the most miserable conditions, wading through burns in spate, splashing through peat-bogs, occasionally sleeping in sheds. On this exercise I first fell foul of my C.O. A lad from Glasgow had told me he was very worried about his sick wife and child. I pleaded with the C.O. to give the lad compassionte leave. He grudgingly consented but the touching story I had listened to turned out to be complete fabrication, and the soldier went absent without leave. This incident naturally did not endear me to the C.O. I soon discovered he was a heavy tippler and that he kept the mess-corporal up till all hours to satisfy his thirst. At the corporal's request, I tackled the C.O. on the subject. At the end of our interview he said, with seeming sincerity, "It is good to have a padre who has the courage to speak his mind" and promised to mend his ways.

A week later I went on leave, at the end of which I was posted to another battalion, fortunately, in the same Mountain Division. I was not surprised to learn that shortly afterwards the gentleman responsible for my posting was reduced from Colonel to Captain, and finally was dismissed the Service. The bottle was his downfall.

Now, our severe high-altitude training, we were told, was in preparation to fight the Nazis occupying Norway. So two winters were spent in the Cairngorms, living in igloos and snowholes. Years from now, perhaps, someone will come across strange pieces of equipment in the high places. For example a snowshoe combined with a short ski, and will wonder how it came to be there, and for what purpose! Let me say that the Knight in Alice in Wonderland would have felt very poorly equipped compared to our lads. We had several different sorts of footwear, ammunition boots, ski boots, boots marching-ski, boots bucheron, and so on. We had sledges and huskies, and climbing gear. And one fantastic creation, snowshoes for mules, thought up by some comedian in Whitehall! But the mules were not amused. I shall never forget the first, and only time, we shod a mule with these monstrosities. The dumb beast patiently submitted to the operation, (without an anaesthetic) but once all four hooves were shod, it kicked the lot into the air and bolted, and that was the end of that. I have never seen a mule so insulted!

Then someone in the deep south designed ski-suits made of denim; all right in theory but when these suits got wet and then froze up, we were virtually encased in suits of armour and could scarcely move. When we tried to bend we crackled!

Despite Whitehall, it was amazing how quickly our men learned to ski, under skilled Norwegian instructors. Thank goodness, we were never called to go into action as ski-troops, carrying heavy, unwieldily rucksacks as well as brens and stens and what have you!

Come Sunday mornings the lads would line up in falling snow, with skis at the ready and I would conduct a short Service, always finishing with "I to the hills will lift mine eyes". The rest of the day would be spent on the high plateaux and speeding down the exhilarating snow-filled corries. All of this, I remember with peculiar pleasure. Our sleeping quarters, though not up to Ritz standards, were surprisingly comfortable in these arctic conditions. We had experimented, unsuccessfully, with four man tents and two man tents and finally with snow-holes and igloos!—Eskimo style. I opted for the snowhole. This consisted of a large hollow sphere, with a sleeping bench for three, the entrance from a tunnel beneath the snow. A blizzard could be raging outside but, snug as hibernating squirrels, we would not be aware of it. These 'billets' would be dug out from a great bank of snow on the hillside, sometimes with half a dozen adjacent, so that it was simple to tunnel from one to the other and thus enjoy sub-arctic social life, great fun!

I have never been able to verify the story in detail but it seems there were several Nazi divisions holding the Norwegian coastline. Had these been released, it might have made all the difference to the Second Front, but they were detained there to repulse any surprise attack by our superbly trained and equipped mountain troops. I was told that we allowed the Nazis to break our code without their knowing it. Thus they were able to pinpoint all our movements, which was the object of the exercise. This kept them from moving out of Norway. If this were true, it was a very clever ruse. But naturally, the men were spoiling for some action which came in a totally unexpected form. We were suddenly told we were to become airborne and *all* our equipment had to be portable. My rucksack, among much else, had to accommodate fifty hymn books, a Communion set and Communion wine. Stationed now in a Deeside village, we had to disguise all our movements so as not to give the slightest clue to the locals, especially the girls. All sorts of devices were resorted to. A Dakota (without wings)! was made to look like a railway truck with horses and mules tied alongside! Actually we were to be first-line reinforcements for Arnhem. We moved south for this and one Sunday morning we saw a great silver armada of planes and gliders, shining in the sun, as they flew over the North Sea. History records the tragedy of that operation, which was intended to shorten the war. We watched a few surviving aircraft returning and knew we were destined for another role. That, we discovered, was to be part of a sea-borne invasion of Walcheren. We crossed from Dover to Ostend in a heavy sea. The buoys marking the mine-clear channel had been washed from their moorings, but we reached Ostend without incident. The night came when we were to make a direct attack on Flushing across the River Scheldt. The C.O. told us the RAF would go in at midnight and bomb the strong Nazi gun positions. In the event, the cloud base was too low for our planes but, said the C.O., the attack will proceed! So we, trained to fight in the high places, were squeezed into battered-down assault boats wearing Mae Wests—irony indeed. I can remember trying to get a few hours sleep before the attack, lying on a mattress of documents and postal orders, in what remained of the shell-blasted post office of Breskens.

Military history books will tell you the rest, how after some days of fierce fighting we captured the town, with the assistance of heavy naval guns some twelve miles distant. I held a Service of Thanksgiving for victory in the damaged Church of St Jakobs.[12]

Meanwhile a Nazi force of perhaps two thousand, held the market town of Middelburg, which one of our Company Commanders, with some sixty men in amphibious vehicles, captured without loss, an astonishing feat when one knows the details.

Now, there are three parallel approaches to Middelburg—the canal, the railway and the road. The road was cleared of mines to a certain breadth marked off for safety, by white tape. After the capture of the town I was motoring up with the major in a jeep. Halfway there we met one of our tanks and it was obvious that we would have to cross the tape into the area not yet cleared of mines. "Now is the time for your to pray" said the major. And I did, fervently, as we crossed the safety line. Nothing happened, and having rounded the tank, we were back on the road again. "So prayer is effective, after all" said the major. "Sometimes Sir" I said, smiling. Yes, Walcheren was quite a story. I was no hero, but I was there.

12. St Jacobs. In Flushing.

BRUSHES WITH ROYALTY

A visit to Sandy was never less than memorable. He was far travelled and had much to tell. he had spent some years in the Argentine, as a specialist in live-stock. Handsome as Apollo, he never married, although once or twice he came near to being ambushed. He was very much in love with a beautiful French girl he had met in France during the first war. His feelings were reciprocated but he lost her address and he gave up all hope of ever seeing her again. But one day he received a telegram from Boulogne from the girl of his heart, saying she would meet him at King's Cross two days later. "Sadly" said Sandy "her arrival coincided exactly with my departure for the Argentine, so we never met. And that was the end of that".

"And was there never anyone else"? I asked. "Yes" he said, "I got to know a very fine lass in South America, but she lived a long distance from me, and we didn't meet often. Once" he said with a smile, looking far back into time, "I rode all through the night to see her, just for a kiss! That about finished my fine horse, and not long after the romance was finished too. She met someone else. Since then I haven't bothered".

Sandy's war record impressed me. He was made a Captain in the first war before he was twenty, and in all he was decorated four times. "Nothing to boast about" he said modestly. "But there *is* something I can boast about" he added. "I have had contact with four of our monarchs in my time". "Does that include our present Queen"? I asked. "It most certainly does. And it had nothing to do with decorating me. I just happened to be in the right place at the right time".

"Tell us about it" said Archie who was also visiting Sandy that evening. "Well" said Sandy "this is exactly what happened, and if you don't believe me, you can confirm it with our gracious Queen herself. I sometimes wonder if she entered the occasion in her diary, if she keeps a diary". "I must remember to ask her the next time I see her" said Archie with a grin. "Well" began Sandy "I was motoring in the West of Scotland with two lady friends. Sisters they were. As I am something of an ornithologist, I thought I'd like to visit the bird sanctuary on the island of Handa. I made contact with a husky highlander who volunteered to row us across, for a small fee of course. It was a lovely day and the crossing was very pleasant. Safely ashore we started to walk to the other side of the island, where the colony of birds were. It was hot and the going was rough. Three quarters of the way across, the girls begged to be left lying in the heather. They would await my return they said. I agreed, continued on my way, and completed my mission. I was thrilled to see, and hear, the thousands of sea birds who had made this their home, lashed as it was on stormy days by the seas rolling in from the Atlantic. Somehow on the way back I missed the girls. Approaching the little beach where we had landed, hoping to find them there, I found instead two gillie-like men spreading rugs on the sand. One of them accosted me somewhat rudely with "What are you doing here? you know you have no right to be here". "As much right as you" I said. "Did you know" said the other "That an order was issued that no-one was to set foot on Handa today"? "Who could give such an order"? I asked. "Her Majesty the Queen" was the reply. "She and the Duke and a few others are coming here for a picnic today. If you don't believe me look—there's the royal launch making its way here right now. You'd better make yourself scarce". "Not I", said I to myself, "I'm one of the Queen's lieges and I'm staying". There was no time for argument. The launch by this time had grounded on the shingly beach some yards from the shore. And there was the Duke of Edinburgh about to wade ashore—without waders. "Can't you go to their assistance"? I said to one of the gillies who were simply standing and staring. Thus prompted he waded out and gave a piggy-back to the Duke to the shore. The other fellow was dumb as they came and made no movement. So what could I do but come to the lady's assistance? I waded out to the launch, took Her Majesty in my arms, and safely deposited her dryshod on the sand and helped her on to a rug. She thanked me graciously, as did the Duke. I bowed and left to join the girls who by this time had arrived, and were watching the scene. "I think I've seen that lady somewhere that you carried ashore so gallantly. Who is she"? said one of my friends. "Take a look" I said. "Gracious me" they said in unison—"It's the Queen". "The very same" I said. So Handa will always have a special place in my book of memory.

"Marvellous" said Archie. "Fancy holding a Queen in your arms! I don't suppose you could cap that" he said, turning to me. "No"

I said "I never made a queen sit down as Sandy did. But I made a Queen stand up". There was an incredulous murmur from both my friends. "Well" I said "she was an ex-queen, the Queen Mother in fact". "That's as near the throne as doesn't matter" said Archie. "But I'll have to hear you before I believe you". Archie was nothing if not sceptical. Sandy reprimanded him with a glare. "Fancy doubting a minister's word"! "Well" said I, "it happened like this". "The Lady in question was the special guest at the opening of a new marine centre. She, in fact, was there to open it. I, as padre to this particular organisation, was there to conduct a Service of Dedication after the plaque had been unveiled. Her Majesty the Queen Mother was sitting on the platform beside the President of the organisation who, if the truth be told, was a bit of a blether. The Service, thankfully, went through without a hitch, until near the very end. After the singing of the last hymn the assembled company, as is the custom, remained standing for the Benediction. The Queen Mother, however, and the aforesaid loquacious President sat down, and started chatting, sotto voce, of course. In the circumstances, I allowed a moments grace, but as the two were still engrossed in conversation, I had to indicate with an upward motion of my hands, that the Queen Mother should stand with the rest of the congregation. She responded immediately, blushing slightly but smiling. The President was a full second slower, and he neither blushed nor smiled. So both were included in the Blessing".

"Well, well" said Archie "fancy giving an order to royalty, but I suppose you had no option. Indeed, you would have been failing in your duty if you had allowed the Lady to sit through the Benediction". "That's right" said Sandy "but I would rather help a Queen to be seated, as I did, rather than order a Queen to stand up, even if you only signed to her to do so". "I may add" I said "that she didn't take it amiss for she spoke to me afterwards making no reference whatsoever either to her own sin of omission or to my sin of presumption. A very, gracious lady indeed".

"By the way" I continued "it was in my offical capacity as a padre that I rubbed shoulders with royalty directly or indirectly. For example, it so happened that the Princess Royal was Colonel of the regiment to which I was attached. And one memorable afternoon she came to tea in the Officers' Mess. By the way I had phoned Annie earlier in the day—she wasn't far away at the time—asking her to come and meet a certain lady. It was forbidden, of course, to mention names on the phone in these days. Annie duly arrived, and was 'presented' but not dressed in her best as she would have been had she known the lady's identity.

Well, during tea I sat next to the Princess Royal and found her very friendly and very shy. She was obviously very interested in the welfare of the men judging by the questions she asked me. Now, it was the days of the strictest rationing but the mess corporal had miraculously produced a number of sumptuous and delicious cakes. The C.O.'s little girl, aged nine, gazed in wonder at all the rare concoctions and suddenly said in a loud voice, to the embarrassment of her father and the rest of us, "And what are the poor soldiers having for *their* tea, daddy"? The Princess relieved the embarrassed silence with a merry laugh and we all thankfully joined in. The day was saved.

"You were stationed on Deeside for a while, I believe" said Sandy. "Were you ever present at the Gillies' Ball at Balmoral"? "I'm afraid not" I replied. "You see the chief guests were the gillies and the soldiers who were then on guard at the Castle. It's a great occasion for them, but you may be interested to know that I once visited Abergeldie Castle where the men on guard were billeted". "It was the day after the Gillies' Ball. I found the young soldiers there over the moon with excitement. Boasting and bragging they were, and with good reason, for they had been dancing with royalty all evening, off and on. What a story they had to tell their girl friends! To have danced with the Queen—my goodness! I noticed one little fellow, however, who was looking very glum. Paring potatoes he was and I was sure he must have been on guard duty the night before when the rest of the lads were enjoying themselves. I was wrong. He had been with the others. Great, I said, you must have enjoyed yourself. Did you have a dance with the Queen? 'No' he said. Or with Princess Elizabeth? 'No' he said—with a strong Glasgow accent. 'I niver got any higher than the Duchess o' Kent'. Never mind, I comforted him. There's always a next time. 'Mebbe aye, an' mebbe no' he replied".

I have conducted Service in Crathie Church but never in the Queen's presence. I was not included among the Elect who were invited to preach there each summer. Those invited also spent the weekend at Balmoral, including friends of mine who had interesting and often amusing stories to tell me about their week-ending with royalty. One such friend was the Moderator of the Church of Scotland the summer he was invited. He has departed, regretfully, without writing his memoirs, but I am sure, wherever he is in the celestial fields, he will not be wroth with me for recording some of the amusing things he told me. On the Sunday afternoon in question he was sitting in the drawing room talking to the King. Princess Margaret, then about fourteen, was present. After a time she understandably got bored with the adult conversation. She walked across to the piano, sat down and started banging out 'Annie get your gun' to the King's obvious embarrassment. He said nothing at the time, however, but next morning when they were walking in the garden he said to my friend, "I'm sorry, Sir, about Margaret's behaviour yesterday afternoon". "There's nothing to apologise for, your Majesty" said my friend. "That was quite a normal thing for a teenager to do". "Quite normal"? said the King. "Are you sure"? "Of course, Sir, quite normal" and the King was greatly relieved to have this judgement on his daughter's behaviour from a high-ranking churchman. As they continued their walk the King said "I have tried without success to get a so-fa copy of the Church of Scotland hymn-book. They must be very scare". "Practically unobtainable at the moment" said my friend. With a twinkle in his eye the King said "Might you not get me a copy—on the black market"? George VI had a fine sense of humour.

At dinner that evening, my friend was seated next the King. After a splendid meal the other people at the table, including some distinguished guests, gradually left, leaving the King and my friend deep in conversation. "We were discussing the Red Dean" said my friend "and the King had his own ideas about that prelate.[13] How long we sat there I can't tell but eventually a footman approached carrying a silver tray on which there was a sheet of paper. Immediately he saw it, the King smiled and said "That'll be my wife telling me it was time I joined the other guests'.—And of course he was right".

As I was leaving the following morning my friend told me "I had a princess kneeling at my feet". "Really" I said. "Oh yes", he

13. Red Dean. Dean of Canterbury during the war. He had leftist tendencies, hence the Red.

continued—"it was not an act of homage. Not even of respect. She was simply examining the silver buckles on my moderatorial shoes".

Another friend, also a guest preacher, became very friendly with the children during his royal weekend. He said to Charles, a small boy at the time, "I would like to send you a book when I get home. What sort of book would you like"? And promptly Charles said "Oh, a book about lions, Sir". Then feeling he hadn't said the right thing to a dignitary of the Church, he corrected himself and said, "No, Sir, a Bible". My friend later sent him a book on lions which he may still possess!

STRICTLY PERSONAL

At my introduction to my highland parish, a famous Scottish preacher told the following story. "A certain minister" he said "kept a dog, a very large, a very ugly dog. So ugly was it that his parishioners thought it was an insult to the cloth, and they decided to ask him to get rid of it. And so a deputation went to the manse and put the matter to him. He was not perturbed". "You know" he said calmly, "I am a great lover of dogs and if I had the money I would have some of the finest dogs obtainable, boizois, afghan hounds and so on. But on the miserable salary you people pay me, I can only afford one composite dog. And this is it, and I intend to keep it". The deputation left with its tail between its legs.

The point the professor was making was that the minister is a composite dog, with a collar to match. He is a man with many parts to play, and many duties to perform, both within and without his parish. I know this from experience. In the same parish I was the pastor, the preacher, Hon. Chaplain to the British Sailors' Society, Director of the Deep Sea Mission, Chaplain to the Sea Cadets, Chaplain to two schools, a mixed secondary school and a private girls' school. There are frequent requests to speak at various functions, to give talks to students and so on. It is not generally known, but with sermons, addresses and talks a minister writes the equivalent of two full-length novels a year. That takes some doing. In addition of course he has to make time to be with his family, of whom he sees far too little. When we first came to a city charge I told Annie I would take her out for coffee every Monday morning. I was able to keep my promise only once in twenty years. Very occasionally we went as a family to a concert or the pictures.

Next to the Bible the most important book in my possession was my diary. Reading the scripture each day was a priority appointment—with God. Then I immediately consulted my diary—to remind myself of my appointments—with man. The Chinese have a proverb—'The strongest memory is weaker than the palest ink'. A wise proverb for a minister to take note of, for a key word in his life is involvement. He is inescapably involved in affairs—spiritual and temporal. He is closely identified with his people in their joys and sorrows, and the various crises in their lives.

His hours of work? He has no union to dictate. We read in Mark's Gospel Chapter One that Jesus must have been involved with people (and God) at least eighteen hours a day. So a minister cannot have a brass plate on his door stating his hours of business—9 to 12 and 2 to 5. He must be accessible twenty four hours a day.

The important part played by a minister's wife in this busy life cannot be exaggerated. She will be the President of the Women's Guild and a Sunday School teacher. She will visit people in their homes and in hospital. She will keep in touch with the old and the housebound. She is, in fact, the minister's unpaid assistant in every department except the pulpit. I am quite certain that any success I may have achieved in my ministry has been largely due to Annie's tact and patience and grace—not to mention her good looks. She was popular with all members of the congregation. I must say I do not know how a priest gets on without a wife.

One close friend, a Roman Catholic priest, confessed to me that he was disappointed in the present Pope's attitude to matrimony and the priesthood. "I was very hopeful that he would relent" said my friend. "In fact I had planned to order a dual-control electric blanket. But now I must pursue my lonely road, unaccompanied to the end".

One thing that used to worry Annie was my occasional solitary ski-trip into the mountains. This may not be an advisable exercise considering the uncertainty of the Scottish hill climate, but my high-altitude winter training in the army had taught me to cope with most emergencies. But I admit I sometimes overdid it when the conditions were really good. I recall one perfect day on the high slopes and in the glistening corries when I was loth to stop although I knew I had a wedding in the late afternoon, some twelve miles away. I cut it very fine and arrived just in time. The bride was already there so I had to conduct the Service wearing my ski-boots and with my robe covering my ski-clothes. I don't think the couple noticed; they had eyes only for each other.

My ski-training stood me in good stead for I was able to visit outlying crofts and farms when deep snow rendered all roads inaccessible. On one occasion I took my rucksack, filled with provisions, to an old lady high up on the hill. I reached the little house with some difficulty. She welcomed me warmly enough, but would have none of the things I had carried so far. "I never accept charity" she said. "I have a girnal full of meal so I'm alright, thank you".

On one occasion I accompanied a local shepherd, also on skis, to look for some snow-stranded sheep and lambs. I carried home two lambs. There's surely something to be said for ministers in highland parishes having skis and knowing how to use them.

On another occasion I was making my homeward way off the hill, ski-shod and in a hurry because the day was short. I had to pass a solitary farmhouse whose tenants did not belong to my flock. I did not stop, but I had been spotted by the farmer's wife who afterwards complained to a friend "The parish minister went past our door yon very stormy night and did not come in. I thought it very uncivil of him. In such weather we would have been glad to see anybody".

One bit of advice I would give to young ministers—be careful not to become involved in financial matters. I recall two elderly sisters whom I visited fairly regularly. To all appearances they were almost on the bread-line, and I would sometimes bring them some of Annie's delectable scones. One day they said they had decided to leave me their money. Looking at the bare kitchen I wondered what they possibly could have saved. Not willing to appear ungrateful I said "But you have a nephew and a niece. Surely you should leave your possessions to them". "But they never come near us" they said. "Even so" I said "they are your own flesh and blood, and they must come first". Rather unwillingly they took my advice. And was I glad? After they died it was discovered that they had hoarded some £28,000 in biscuit tins, besides various shares. You can imagine what would have been said by the relatives, and others, had I been the sole legatee. Mind you I could have done with a few thousand pounds from these biscuit tins. I should mention that they did leave me £100, the old dears.

Nor should a minister, married or unmarried, become romantically involved, or even appear to be. I knew one young bachelor minister, very good looking and eminently eligible, who was almost pursued by his choir girls. Sadly outnumbered and greatly embarrassed he saw no way out but to leave for another parish. I said to him afterwards—"I thought there was safety in numbers"! "Perhaps" he replied "but I thought there was greater safety in EXODUS"!

Ulysses said "I am a part of all that I have met". A minister can say the same. If his experiences were woven into a tapestry the pattern would be a very complex one and a veritable kaleidoscope of colour.